Easy Reader Level B

Win with Sounds

Karen E. Williams

This book belongs to:

____

Name

____

Date

Easy Reader Publishing
Telephone: (876) 830-6516 (Text/Whatsapp)
Email: easyreader14@gmail.com

ISBN 978 976 96386 0 0
Cover design: Anthony Smith
Cover photo courtesy of Ebony Williams Parris (Philadelphia, Pennsylvania)
Illustrator: Jodie-Ann Dunn
Editor: Concheta Wilson
© September 2019 by Karen E. Williams

Acknowledgements
The author wishes to thank participating schools and an individual for piloting this book in Jamaica:

Kingston
- ✓ St. Margaret's Human Resource Centre

Clarendon
- ✓ Birdlyn Murray, private tutor

St. Catherine
- ✓ Ascot High
- ✓ Ascot Primary
- ✓ Ebony Vale Baptist Basic
- ✓ Friendship Primary
- ✓ Linstead Primary and Junior High
- ✓ St. John's Primary
- ✓ Stewart Early Childhood

St. Thomas
- ✓ Paul Bogle Junior High
- ✓ Robert Lightbourne High

NOTES TO THE TEACHER AND OTHER USERS

This book is the third in the *Easy Reader Series*. It is intended to help the learner to learn short vowel sounds with twenty-six of the most common consonant-vowel-consonant words, the first 100 of Fry's High-Frequency Words and Picture Nouns. The Table of Content shows the range of skills that the book covers.

How to use this book:
- ✓ The instructor should have an understanding of Direct Instruction, The 5 Components of Reading and Vygotsky's Zone of Proximal Development for 100% success rate.
- ✓ All High-Frequency Words are in red. They only appear in this colour when first mentioned.
- ✓ In each section, the vowel and ending sound of focus is colour coded to assist the learner in recall. However, in the Speed Drills all letters are in black.
- ✓ Each unit should be taught using various strategies. The learner should master all words to gain mastery for reading.
- ✓ The contents are spiral, providing learners with the opportunity to encounter the combination of consonants and vowels multiple times.

✓ Speed Drills are inserted to increase fluency. Have the learner underline the vowel sound in the phonetic speed drill sections. Have them practice reading each word independently to prepare for the one-minute speed drill.
✓ At the end of each unit there is an assessment of words. The criterion for each assessment is found at the end of each list.
✓ The Progress Report Assessment found at the back of the book records the child's progress. The speed at which the learner read each word can be recorded using the following criteria: **S**-Slow, **M**- Moderate and **F**-Fast.
✓ The final assessment is done in the form of a regular in-school reading assessment to assess the learner's reading competency at the completion of this book level.

Layout of Content

Sample Introductory page

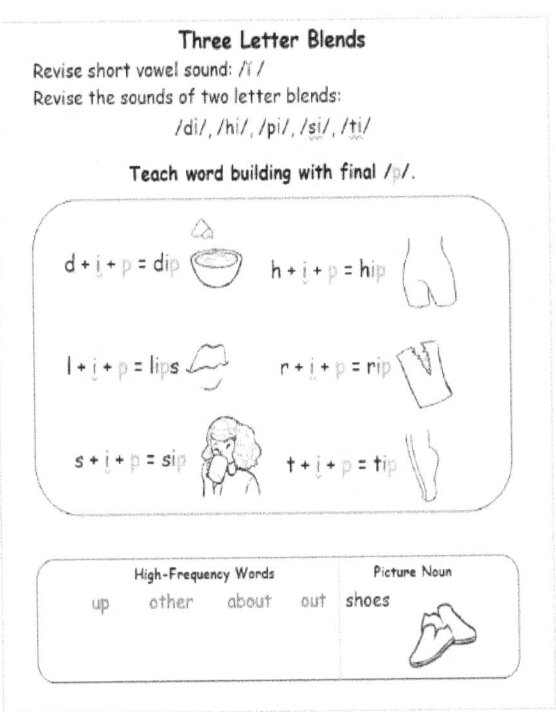

Sample Reading Passage

Table of Contents

	Page
Pre-Assessment	1

Unit 1 Short Vowel /a/

	Page
3-letter blends with final /t/	2
Rat	3
Pat	5
Speed Drills	6
3-letter blends with final /d/	7
Dad	8
Pat	8
Dad and the Lad	8
Speed Drills	9
3-letter blends with final /n/	10
The Van	11
And, Hand	12
Can	13
Speed Drills	14
3-letter blends with final /p/	15
Homophones	16
Tap	17
Speed Drills	18
3-letter blends with final /m/	19

	Page
Pam and Sam	20
Pam and Sam Can Play	21
Speed Drills	22
3-letter blends with final /g/	23
Tags on Bags	24
Homophones	25
The Fat Man	26
Wag	26
The House	27
Speed Drills	28
Assessment 1	29

Unit 2 Short Vowel /e/

	Page
3-letter blends with final /t/	31
Sentences with –et Words	32
The Jet	33
Speed Drills	34
3-letter blends with final /n/	35
I Can	36
Speed Drills	37
3-letter blends with final /d/	39
Sentences With –ed Words	40

Table of Contents

	Page
Red	41
His and Is	42
This and That	43
Speed Drills	44
3-letter blends with final /g/	46
Sentences With –eg Words	47
Meg	48
Speed Drills	49
Twin Consonant Ending /ll/	51
Sentences With –ll Words	52
The Bell	53
Ten Men	54
Speed Drills	55
Assessment 2	57
Unit 3 Short Vowel /i/	
3-letter blends with final /t/	59
Sentences With –it Words	60
Hit and It	61
Keep Fit	62
Speed Drills	63
3-letter blends with final /n/	65

	Page
Sentences With –in Words	66
In and Inn	67
Days	68
Speed Drills	69
3-letter blends with final /g/	71
Sentences With –ig Words	72
Colours at a House	73
Win	74
Speed Drills	75
3-letter blends with final /d/	77
Sentences With –id Words	78
Speed Drills	79
3-letter blends with final /x/	81
Sentences With –ix Words	82
Mother and Father	83
Speed Drills	84
Twin Consonant Ending /ll/	86
Sentences With –ill Words	87
The Hill	88
There and Their	89
Speed Drills	90

Table of Contents

Page

3-letter blends with final /p/........ 93

Sentences With -ip Words........... 94

Tip.......... 95

The Pig.......... 96

Dad and I.......... 97

Speed Drills........... 98

Assessment 3........... 101

Unit 4 Short Vowel /o/

3-letter blends with final /t/....... 104

Sentences With -ot Words.......... 105

The Cat With the Dot.................. 106

These.......... 107

Speed Drills.......... 108

3-letter blends with final /g/....... 111

The Hogs in the Fog.................. 112

3-letter blends with final /p/....... 114

Hop to the Top.................. 115

3-letter blends with final /x/...... 116

The Fox and the Box.................. 117

Speed Drills........... 119

Assessment 4........... 123

Page

Unit 5 Short Vowel /u/

3-letter blends with final /t/....... 127

The Little Hut.................. 128

If You Could.......... 129

Get Up.......... 130

3-letter blends with final /p/....... 131

A Pup.......... 132

3-letter blends with final /n/........ 133

Mum and the Nun.................. 134

Twin Consonant Ending /zz/........... 136

Buzz the Bee.......... 137

Saturday.......... 139

The Bad Rat.................. 140

Speed Drills.................. 145

Assessment 5.................. 149

Final Assessment.................. 153

Oral Scoring Rubric.......... 156

Final Assessment Scoring Sheet.. 158

Lesson Plan Guide.......... 159

Pre-Assessment Record Sheets.. 164

Assessment Progress Sheets......... 165

Pre Assessment Sheet

Name: _____________________   Date: _______________

Look at each word and read what it says.

1. fat	11. nap
2. Tim	12. doll
3. pen	13. mix
4. jet	14. yell
5. Zac	15. wig
6. quit	16. lid
7. vet	17. gun
8. rip	18. box
9. cut	19. sat
10. kit	20. hen

Please see page 162 for individual scoring sheet.
Please see page 163 for group record sheet.

Easy Reader Level B   1

Unit 1 Short Vowel /A/
Three letter Blends

Revise short vowel sound: /ă/

Revise the sounds of two letter blends:

/ba/, /ca/, /fa/, /ha/, /ma/, /ra/, /sa/

Teach word building with final /t/.

b + a + t = bat

f + a + t = fat

c + a + t = cat

m + a + t = mat

h + a + t = hat

s + a + t = sat

r + a + t = rat

High-Frequency Word	Picture Noun
the	boy

Rat

the rat	the hat	the mat

the bat	the bat	the fat rat

The cat sat.	The fat boy	The fat bat

The fat rat sat.	The fat cat sat.	The fat boy sat.

Three Letter Blends

Revise short vowel sound: /ă/

Revise the sounds of two letter blends:/pa/

Teach word building with final /t/.

High-Frequency Word	Picture Noun	Generative Sight Words
and	girl	play run

Easy Reader Level B

The girl

Pat

The boy and the girl

The boy and the girl play.

The boy and Pat run.

Pat and the cat run.

The cat and Pat run.

The fat boy and Pat play.

The fat rat and the boy sat.

Speed Drills

Read these words many times. Have someone time you. See how many words you can read in a minute.

rat	sat	Pat	pat	mat
bat	cat	fat	hat	

the	and	can	play	girl
run	boy			

1st Reading: _______ words in a minute

2nd Reading: _______ words in a minute

3rd Reading: _______ words in a minute

Three Letter Blends

Revise short vowel sound: /ă/

Revise the sounds of two letter blends:

/ba/, /da /, /ha /, /la /, /ma/

Teach word building with final /d/.

d + a + d = dad

m + a + d = mad

s + a + d = sad

l + a + d = lad

b + a + d = bad

h + a + d = had

High-Frequency Words	Picture Noun	Generative Sight Word
A to is a	 man	like

Dad

Dad.

Dad can run.

The lad can play.

Dad and a lad like to play.

A lad and dad like to run and play.

Pat

Pat.

Pat is a girl.

Pat can play.

Pat can run.

Dad and the Lad

Dad is a man.

A lad is a boy.

Dad had a mat.

Dad and the lad sat.

The dad can play.

The lad can run.

Easy Reader Level B

Speed Drills

Read these words many times. Have someone time you. See how many words you can read in a minute.

dad	mad	sad	lad	bad
bat	sat	Pat	pat	mat
had	cat	fat	hat	rat

run	boy	is	man	like
the	and	can	play	girl
to	A	a		

1st Reading: _______ words in a minute

2nd Reading: _______ words in a minute

3rd Reading: _______ words in a minute

Three Letter Blends

Revise short vowel sound: /ă/

Revise the sounds of two letter blends:

/ca/, /fa/, /ma/, /na/, /pa/, /ra/, /va/

Teach word building with final /n/.

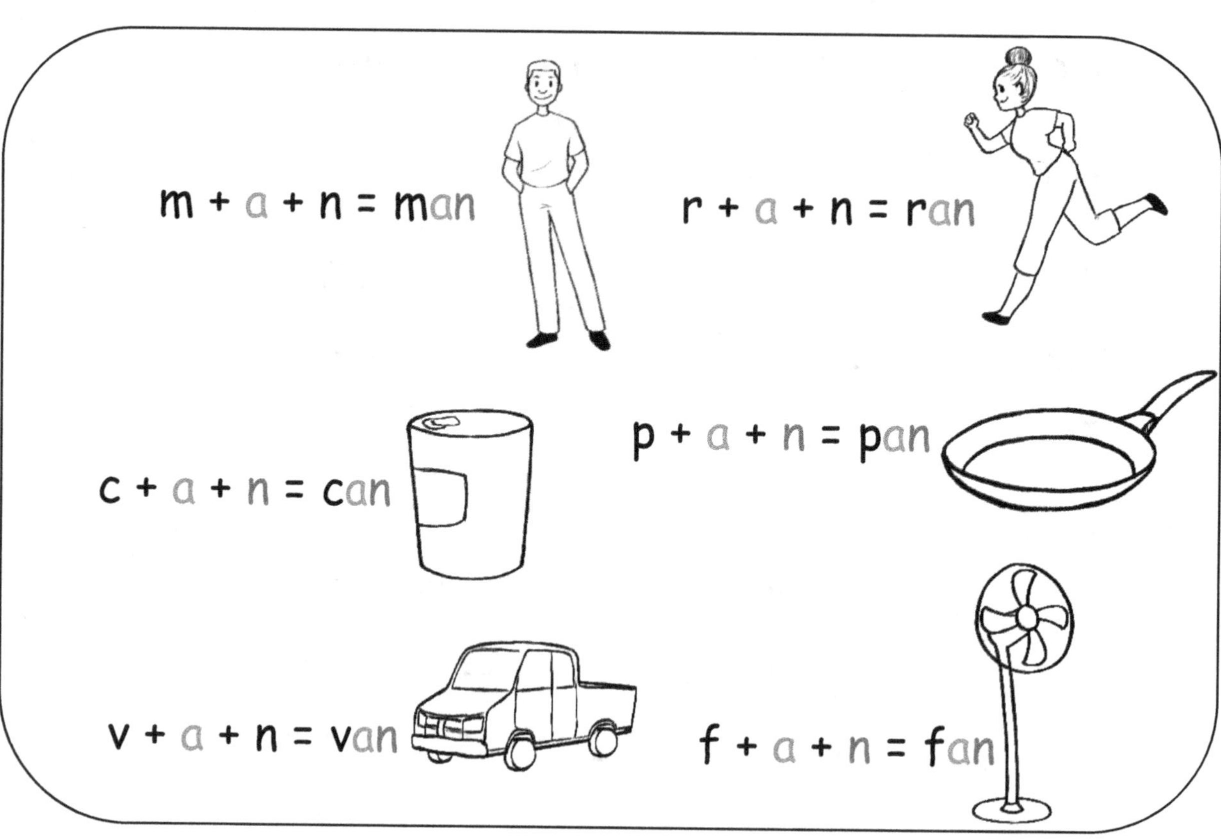

High-Frequency Words	Picture Noun	Generative Sight Words
in you	woman	want see

The Van

A can see a man.
Dad is a man.
Dad is a big man!
Dad ran in the van.

You can see a fan.
The fan is in the van.
You like the fan.
The woman and a cat like the fan.

The girl can see a can.
A can is in the van.
A pan is in the van.

Pat can see the pan.
A can is in the pan.
The girl can see the can.
You want the pan in the van.
A can, a fan, a pan and a man is in the van.

And, Hand

and

A woman and the cat can play.

hand

A hand

Ann

Ann.

Ann is a woman.

Ann can play.

Ann can run.

an

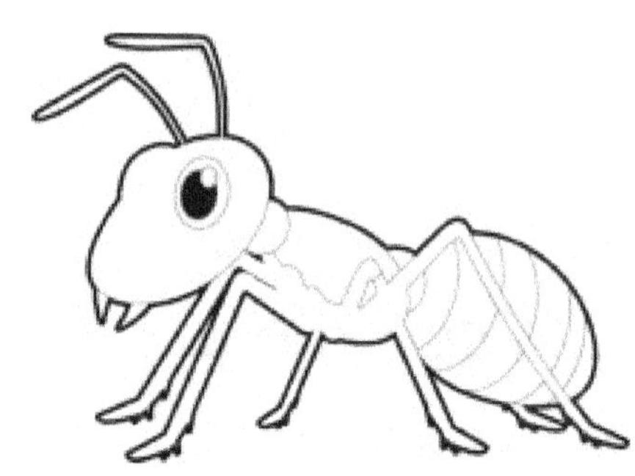

I can see an ant.

I can see an ant in the van.

I can see an ant in the pan.

Easy Reader Level B

Can

The boy can run.

Pat can play.

The man can run and play.

The woman can run and play.

The cat can play with the can.

The woman can play with the can.

The woman and the man can play with the can. 

Speed Drills

Read these words many times. Have someone time you. See how many words you can read in a minute.

bat	rat	man	pan	van
can	fan	fat	hat	mat
dad	cat	Pat	pat	bad
had	sat	sad	lad	mad
ran				

woman	want	see	in	you
to	A	a	play	girl
the	and	can	man	like
run	boy	is		

1st Reading: _______ words in a minute

2nd Reading: _______ words in a minute

3rd Reading: _______ words in a minute

Easy Reader Level B

Three Letter Blends

Revise short vowel sound: /ă/

Revise the sounds of two letter blends:

/ca/, /la/, /ma/, /na/, /ra/, /ta/, /wa/

Teach word building with final /p/.

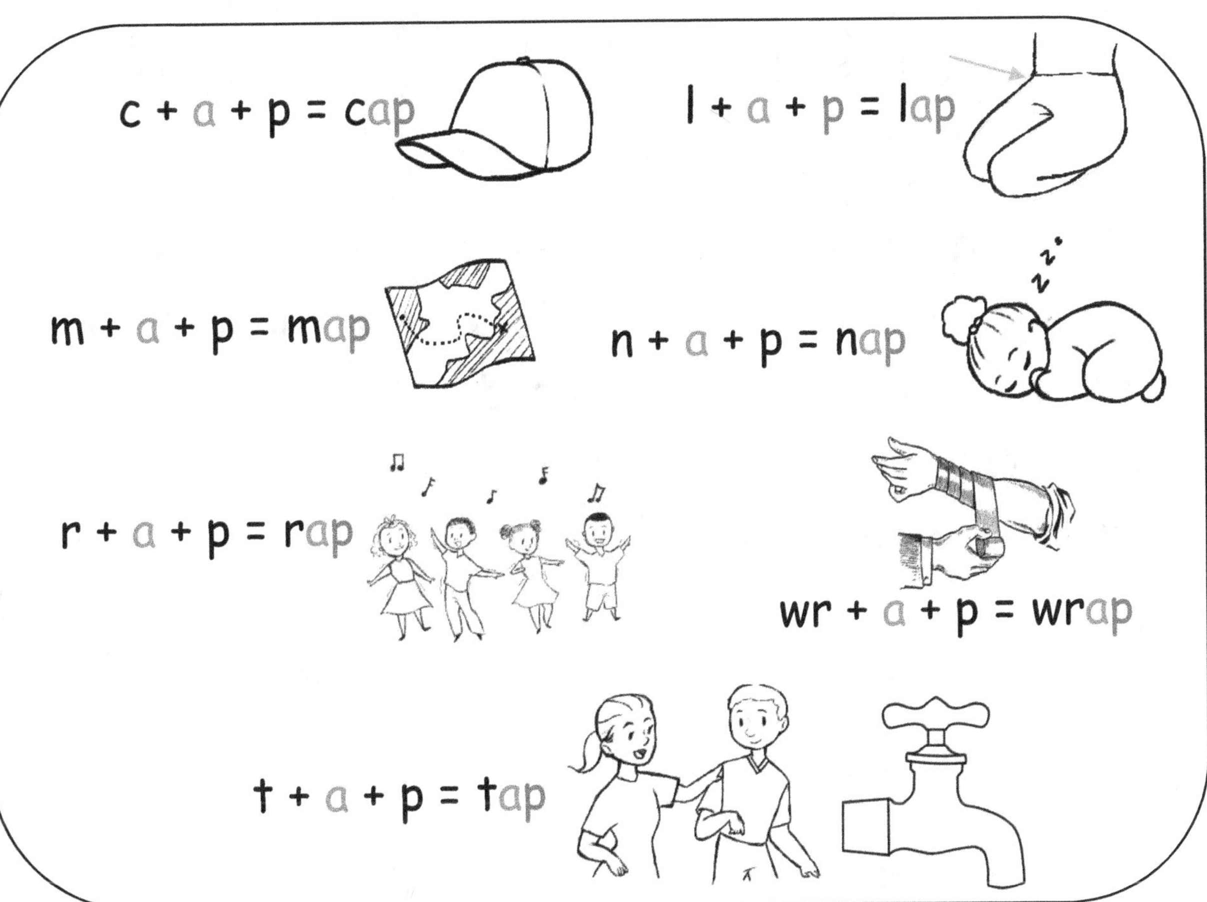

High-Frequency Words	Picture Noun	Generative Sight Words
that it	baby	look little

Homophones

Rap

A boy and a girl can rap.

Dad and Pat can rap.

Dad and Sam can rap.

A man can rap.

A woman sat and rap.

Wrap

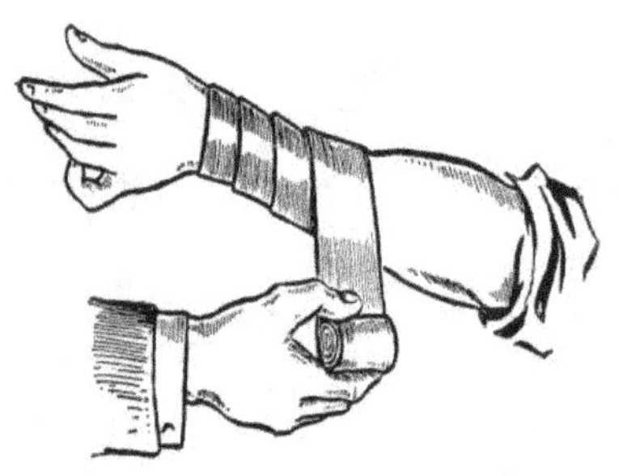

Dad can wrap a hand.

The woman can wrap my hand.

At

Look at Pat.

Pat can look at the cat.

Hat

The cat and the dog play with the hat.

Easy Reader Level B

Tap

Look at the tap.

I can see the tap.

That is a little tap.

It is a little tap.

A baby can tap.

A baby can tap the mat.

The boy can tap.

The boy can tap the sad cat.

The woman can tap the cap.

The woman can tap the cap in the van.

Pat can tap.

Pat can tap the little cat.

Speed Drills

Read these words many times. Have someone time you. See how many words you can read in a minute.

dad	cat	Pat	pat	rat
can	fan	sad	lad	bad
ran	mad	fat	hat	mat
lap	cap	map	nap	tap
rap	wrap	man	pan	van
had	sat	bat		

run	boy	is	look	little
the	and	can	man	like
to	A	a	play	girl
woman	want	see	in	you

1st Reading: _______ words in a minute

2nd Reading: _______ words in a minute

3rd Reading: _______ words in a minute

Three Letter Blends

Revise short vowel sound: /ă/

Revise the sounds of two letter blends:

/ha/, / ja/, /pa/, /sa/

Teach word building with final /m/.

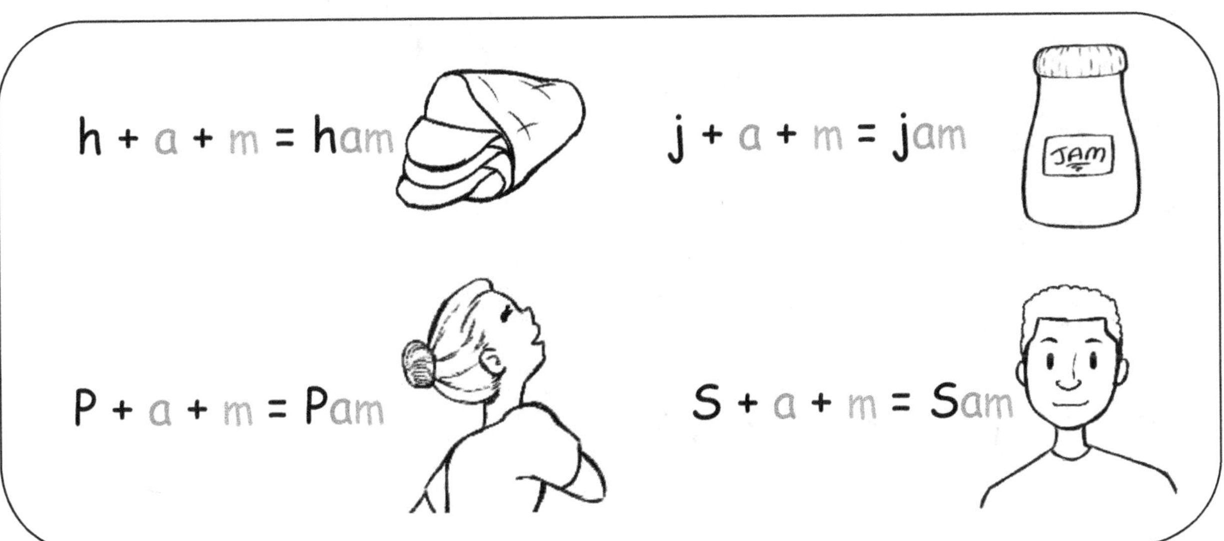

High-Frequency Words	Picture Noun	Generative Sight Word
he was	ball	pretty

Pam and Sam

Pam is a girl.

Pam is a little girl.

Pam is pretty.

Pam is a pretty, little girl.

Sam is a boy.

He is a little boy.

Sam is sad.

He is a sad, little boy.

Easy Reader Level B

Pam and Sam Can Play

Look at the ball.

The ball is pretty.

The ball is little.

Pam and Sam want to play.

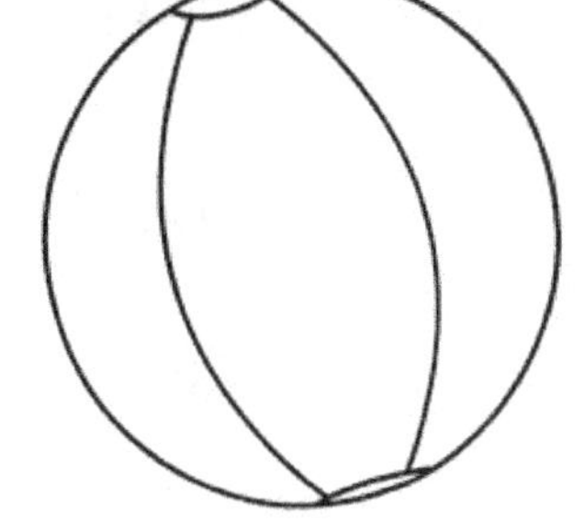

Look at the jam.

Sam had jam.

He had jam.

Pam and Sam want the jam.

Pat can rap with Pam and Sam.

Pam and Sam can rap and play.

You can rap.

Pam and Sam rap in the van.

A man is in the van.

He was mad.

Speed Drill

Read these words many times. Have someone time you. See how many words you can read in a minute.

had	sat	bat	hat	van
ran	mad	fat	lad	tap
rap	wrap	man	nap	mat
lap	cap	map	pan	ham
dad	cat	Pat	pat	bad
can	fan	sad	rat	Sam
jam	Pam			

ball	you	pretty	he	was
run	boy	is	look	little
the	and	can	man	like
to	A	a	play	girl
woman	want	see	in	

1st Reading: _________ words in a minute

2nd Reading: _________ words in a minute

3rd Reading: _________ words in a minute

Easy Reader Level B

Three Letter Blends

Revise short vowel sound: /ă/

Revise the sounds of two letter blends:

/ba/, /ra/, /ta/, /wa/

Teach word building with final /g/.

b + a + g = bag

r + a + g = rag

t + a + g = tag

w + a + g = wag

High-Frequency Words	Picture Noun	Generative Sight Words
for on are	dog	big funny house

Tags on Bags

A bag and a tag.

A little tag.

A little bag.

A little tag is on the little bag.

Pam can see the pretty tag on the little bag.

Pat can see the pretty tag on the bag.

The pretty bag is for Pam.

Pat is sad.

Pam and dad are sad for Pat.

Dad and Pam pat Pam.

The woman can look for a rag for Pat.

The rag is little.

Pam and Pat look at the rag on the big bag.

Easy Reader Level B

Homophones

See

The cat can see you.

sea

Dan and Sam look at the sea.

Pam and Sam want to play in the sea.

The Fat Man

The fat man sat.

The fat man sat on the mat.

The fat man ran.

The fat man can jump and play.

The fat man sat on a big van.

Wag

Wag.

The funny dog and the big bag.

A funny dog with a little rag!

The House

The baby can see the house.

The house is big.

The house is pretty.

Dad had a van at the house.

Sam had a cat at the house.

Pam had a little dog at the house.

The dog and the cat jump and play at the house.

The baby can play at the house.

Speed Drill

Read these words many times. Have someone time you. See how many words you can read in a minute.

had	sat	bat	rat	wag
dad	cat	Pat	pat	van
rap	wrap	man	pan	tap
lap	cap	map	nap	bad
can	fan	sad	lad	mat
ran	mad	fat	hat	ham
bag	rag	tag	jam	
Pam	Sam			

woman	want	see	in	you
to	A	a	play	girl
the	and	can	man	like
run	boy	is	look	little
dog	jump	house	funny	was
ball	pretty	he	big	

1st Reading: _______ words in a minute

2nd Reading: _______ words in a minute

3rd Reading: _______ words in a minute

Easy Reader Level B

Phonetic Words Assessment 1

Name: _________________________   Date: _______________

Read the words.

_man	_tap	_cap	_hat	_bad
_fat	_ Pam	_ham	_lad	_rap
_jam	_tag	_fan	_pan	_sat
_rag	_bat	_cat	_pat	_mat
_bag	_can	_rat	_wag	_mad
_sad	_dad	_van	_had	_lap
_Pat	_map	_nap	_ran	

Score

____

34

31-34 words correct: **Excellent**
25-30 words correct: **Satisfactory**
17-24 words correct: **Needs Improvement**
1-16 words correct: **Re-teach the unit**

High Frequency Words Assessment 1

Name: ___________________________   Date: _________________

Read the words.

_that	_he	_you	_is	_was
_it	_in	_the	_and	_to
_a	_for	_on	_are	

Score

1-14 words correct: **Excellent**
Drill and practice until all words are memorized.

______
14

Unit 2 Short Vowel /E/
Three Letter Blends

Revise short vowel sound: /ĕ/

Revise two letter blends:

/ge/, /je/, /le/, /ne/, /pe/, /se/, /te/, /ve/, /we/, /ye/

Teach word building with final /t/.

High-Frequency Words	Picture Noun	Generative Sight Words
as with of	train	Sunday help work

Sentences with -et words

Pat can see a jet.

Pam can get a train.

The net is as little as the dog.

The girl is wet.

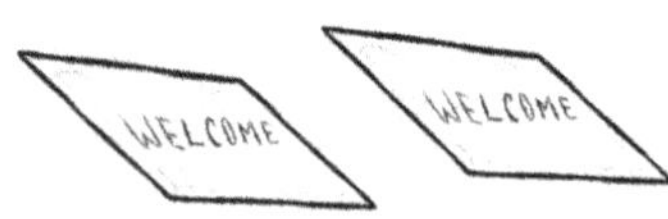

One set of mats are in the jet.

Sam can get to play.

Let the vet help you with the work.

The vet can see the pet.

Easy Reader Level B

The Jet

Is the jet on the mat yet?

Look Sam can see the jet!

It is a big jet!

The big jet is pretty.

Sam can get in the big jet.

The pets get on the big jet.

The pets are in the big jet on the wet net!

Dan met Pat and Pam in the big jet.

On Sunday, Dan can get in the big jet with dad and

Sam.

Speed Drill

Read these words many times. Have someone time you. See how many words you can read in a minute.

ran	mad	fat	hat	mat
can	fan	sad	lad	tap
vet	yet	get	let	van
lap	cap	map	nap	bad
rap	wrap	man	pan	wag
bag	rag	tag	pat	wet
set	jet	net	pet	bat
dad	cat	Pat	rat	sat
had				

A	a	play	big	to
and	can	man	girl	the
ball	of	pretty	he	you
boy	is	look	like	run
dog	jump	house	funny	was
help	work	Sunday	in	little
woman	want	see		

1st Reading: _______ words in a minute

2nd Reading: _______ words in a minute

3rd Reading: _______ words in a minute

Easy Reader Level B

Three Letter Blends

Revise short vowel sound: /ĕ/

Revise the sounds of two letter blends:

/he/, /me/, /pe/, /te/

Teach word building with final /n/.

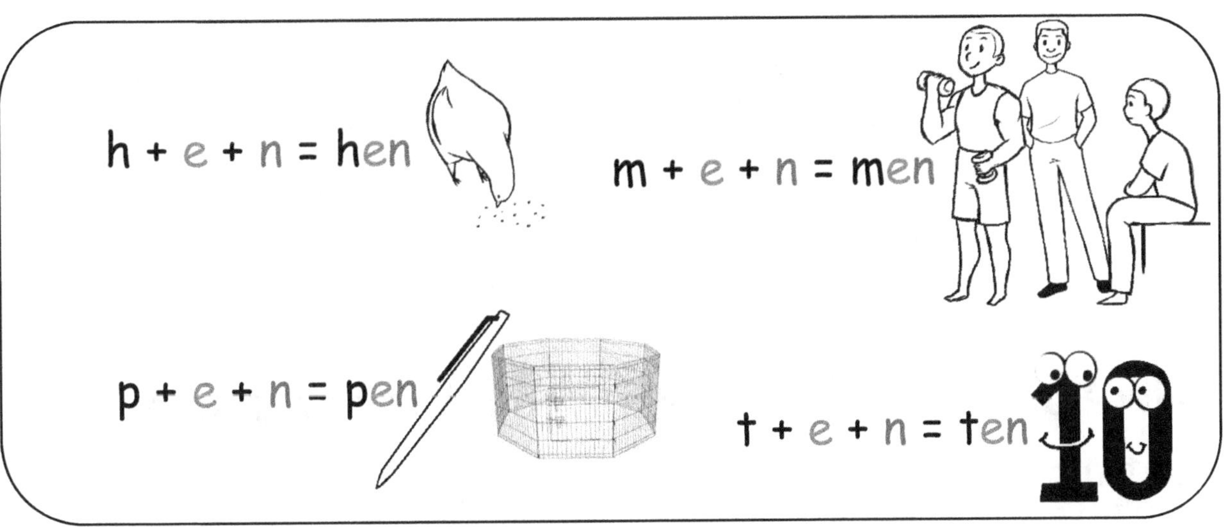

High-Frequency Words	Picture Noun	Generative Sight Words
they I at	game	Monday keep here

I Can

Jen can see a big hen. Jen wants to keep the big fat hen.

 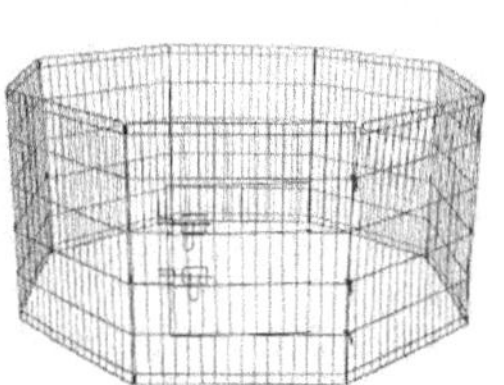

Here are the men at the pen. On Monday, the men sat at the pen.

Ben and Ken look at the pen. They want to keep the pen for dad.

 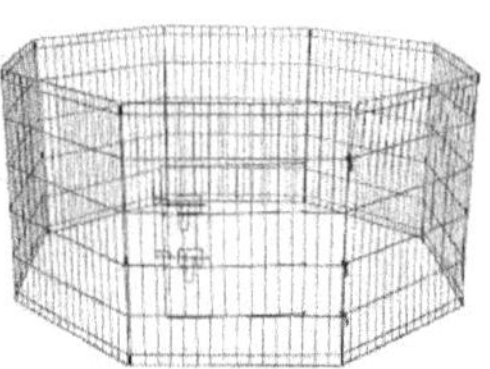

I am at the pen. I want to play a game with Ben at the pen.

Easy Reader Level B

Speed Drill

Read these words many times. Have someone time you. See how
many words you can read in a minute.

bag	rag	tag	rat	hen
can	fan	sad	pet	mat
dad	cat	Pat	pen	wag
had	sat	bat	pat	men
lap	cap	map	pan	van
ran	mad	fat	nap	bad
rap	wrap	man	let	wet
set	jet	net	lad	tap
ten	yet	get	hat	vet

1st Reading: _______ words in a minute

2nd Reading: _______ words in a minute

3rd Reading: _______ words in a minute

Speed Drill

Read these words many times. Have someone time you. See how many words you can read in a minute.

A	jump	play	big	to
and	can	man	girl	the
ball	is	pretty	he	you
boy	a	look	like	run
help	work	house	funny	was
woman	want	Sunday	in	little
I	of	see	Monday	game
here	keep			

1st Reading: _______ words in a minute

2nd Reading: _______ words in a minute

3rd Reading: _______ words in a minute

Three Letter Blends

Revise short vowel sound: /ĕ/

Revise the sounds of two letter blends:

/be/, /pe/, /de/, /fe/, /le/, /ne/, /te/, /re/, /we/

Teach word building with final /d/.

High-Frequency Words	Picture Noun	Generative Sight Words
be this have his	toy	Tuesday walk

Sentences with -ed words

This is a little bed. A toy is on the little bed.

Sam fed his hen on Tuesday.

Dad led the dog for a walk on Tuesday.

Dad had to wed Ann. Dad can wed Ann at the big, red house.

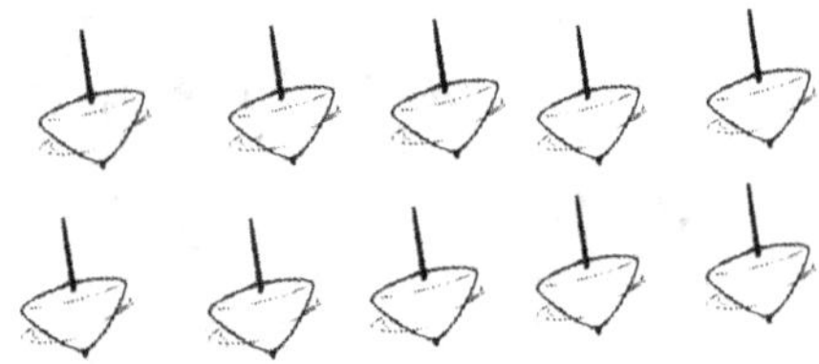

Ned and Ted have ten toys.

Ned and Ted like to be with Ann.

Red

I have a pet hen.

Red is a pet hen.

Red can run and jump.

Red can play with Pat.

On Sunday, Red sat on a bed.

On Monday, I fed Red in the pen.

I can read to Red on Tuesday.

Red is a funny pet hen.

I can play with the funny red hen.

His **and Is**

Pam is a girl.

Pam is a little girl.

Sam is a boy.

He is a big boy.

His

This is Sam.

I can see his bag.

His bag is big.

Easy Reader Level B

This and That

This house is big.

That house is little.

Speed Drill

Read these words many times. Have someone time you. See how many words you can read in a minute.

vet	yet	get	let	tap
rap	wrap	man	pan	bad
Ned	Ted	wed	rat	men
had	sat	bat	pen	hen
bag	rag	tag	hat	wet
ran	mad	fat	pet	mat
set	jet	net	lad	wag
can	fan	sad	pat	red
dad	cat	Pat	fed	van
lap	cap	map	nap	led
ten	bed			

1st Reading: _______ words in a minute

2nd Reading: _______ words in a minute

3rd Reading: _______ words in a minute

Speed Drill

Read these words many times. Have someone time you. See how many words you can read in a minute.

woman	want	see	Monday	game
read	be	this	have	toy
help	work	I	walk	little
dog	jump	Sunday	of	was
boy	is	house	funny	run
ball	can	look	like	you
and	a	pretty	he	the
A	in	man	girl	keep
play	big	to	here	

1st Reading: _______ words in a minute

2nd Reading: _______ words in a minute

3rd Reading: _______ words in a minute

Three Letter Blends

Revise short vowel sound: /ĕ/

Revise the sounds of two letter blends:

/be/, /le/, /me/, /pe/

Teach word building with final /g/.

High-Frequency Words	Picture Noun	Generative Sight Words
from or one	two 2	Wednesday book

Easy Reader Level B

  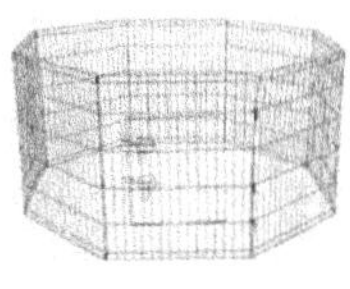

The man can beg dad for a pet.

Dad can get a pet from the pen.

I can see one leg.

I can get one egg or the ham.

 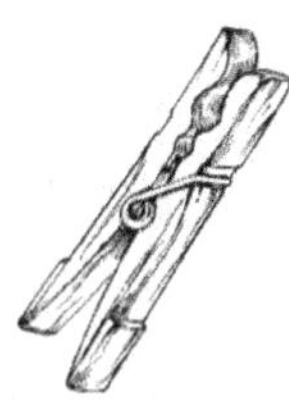

Meg is a pretty girl.

Meg is the pretty girl with the peg.

Meg

This is Meg. Meg is a girl. I want to read from a big book with Meg.

Meg likes to read big books.

I can look at pretty the mats as Meg reads.

Meg likes to play with the dog, Max.

She plays on a Wednesday with the dog, Max.

Max jumps on his leg when he plays with Meg.

Meg and Pam beg Dad to get the toy for Max.

I like to read and play with Meg and Max.

Easy Reader Level B

Speed Drill

Read these words many times. Have someone time you. See how many words you can read in a minute.

Ned	Ted	wed	Meg	beg
bag	rag	tag	pen	hen
can	fan	sad	lad	mat
dad	cat	Pat	pat	wag
set	jet	net	pet	wet
lap	cap	map	nap	van
rap	wrap	man	pan	bad
ten	bed	led	fed	red
vet	yet	get	let	tap
ran	mad	fat	hat	men
leg	peg	egg	rat	bat
had	sat			

1ˢᵗ Reading: _______ words in a minute

2ⁿᵈ Reading: _______ words in a minute

3ʳᵈ Reading: _______ words in a minute

Speed Drill

Read these words many times. Have someone time you. See how many words you can read in a minute.

woman	want	see	Monday	game
read	be	this	have	toy
keep	here	I	walk	little
help	work	Sunday	in	was
dog	jump	house	funny	run
boy	is	look	like	you
ball	can	pretty	he	the
and	a	man	girl	to
A	or	play	big	of
from	one	book	Wednesday	

1st Reading: _______ words in a minute

2nd Reading: _______ words in a minute

3rd Reading: _______ words in a minute

Easy Reader Level B

Twin Consonant Ending

Revise short vowel sound: /ĕ/

Revise the sounds of two letter blends:

/be/, /fe/, /me/, /ne/, /se/, /te/, /we/, /ye/

Teach word building with final /ll/.

b + e + ll = bell

f + e + ll = fell 

M + e + ll = Mell

N + e + ll = Ne

s + e + ll = sell

t + e + ll = tell 

w + e + ll = well

y + e + ll = yell 

High-Frequency Words	Picture Noun	Generative Sight Words
by words but	tree	Thursday

Sentences with -ell words

They can play with the bell in the house.

Pat likes to sell.

Dan fell from the tree.

Ken and Ben can go by the well with dad.

They had to tell dad.

The men yell bad words at dad. Dad was mad!

Let Mell and Nell help Dad.

Easy Reader Level B

The Bell

I can see a bell.

This is a big bell!

The bell is at the well.

Nell and Mell want the big bell for Sam.

Nell fell with the bell by the well.

Nell and Sam help Nell to get up.

Dad yells at the lad as Nell fell at the well with the bell.

Nell and Dad tell Pam to sell the bell.

On Thursday, I had to sell the bell.

Dad likes the bell but he had to sell the bell or be mad.

Ten Men

Jen, Ken and Ben sat with ten funny men on Sunday.

Nell sat with the ten funny men on Monday.

The ten funny men ran to the van on Tuesday.

The ten funny men ran and sat on the van on Wednesday.

The ten funny men can play a game with the hen in the pen.

Mell can jump and play with the ten funny men.

The ten funny men had to go to the big, pretty house.

The ten funny men look at the cat in the house.

Easy Reader Level B

Speed Drill

Read these words many times. Have someone time you. See how many words you can read in a minute.

bag	rag	tag	pen	hen
bell	sell	well	fell	tell
can	fan	sad	lad	mat
dad	cat	Pat	pat	wag
had	sat	bat	rat	men
lap	cap	map	nap	van
leg	peg	egg	Meg	beg
Ned	Ted	wed	hat	bad
ran	mad	fat	pan	wet
rap	jet	net	pet	red
set	bed	led	fed	tap
ten	yet	get	let	Nell
vet	wrap	man	Mell	yell

1st Reading: _________ words in a minute

2nd Reading: _________ words in a minute

3rd Reading: _________ words in a minute

Speed Drill

Read these words many times. Have someone time you. See how many words you can read in a minute.

was	funny	dog	big	to
toy	have	read	girl	the
Thursday	like	boy	he	you
run	walk	words	house	jump
A	in	help	I	here
little	Monday	woman	look	is
game	or	one	see	want
from	can	by	Sunday	work
book	a	pretty	this	be
ball	play	man	Wednesday	tree
and				

1st Reading: _______ words in a minute

2nd Reading: _______ words in a minute

3rd Reading: _______ words in a minute

Easy Reader Level B

Phonetic Words Assessment 2

Name: ___________________________   Date: _______________

Read the words.

_wet	_bat	_fed	_bad	_man
_vet	_beg	_red	_cat	_mat
_ten	_bell	_sell	_hat	_men
_set	_can	_hen	_lad	_Nell
_sad	_dad	_Mell	_let	_fan
_rag	_jet	_tag	_mad	_leg
_Pat	_lap	_Ned	_led	_map
_Meg	_pan	_nap	_Pam	_rap
_jam	_pen	_had	_pat	_sat
_ham	_ran	_van	_peg	_well
_fell	_tap	_rat	_pet	_net
_fat	_Ted	_wag	_tell	_bed
_egg	_wed	_get	_cap	_yet
_bag	_yell			

Score

___67___

60-67 words correct: **Excellent**
51-59 words correct: **Satisfactory**
34-50 words correct: **Needs Improvement**
1-33 words correct: **Re-teach the unit**

High Frequency Words Assessment 2

Name: _____________________   Date: _______________

Read the words.

_to	_he	_his	_have	_words
_the	_is	_for	_I	_or
_of	_you	_are	_at	_one
_in	_was	_they	_from	_on
_and	_that	_as	_be	_had
_a	_it	_with	_this	_by
_but				

Score

____

31

28-31 words correct: **Excellent**

Drill until all words are memorized.

                                        Easy Reader Level B

Unit 3 Short Vowel /I/
Three Letter Blends

Revise short vowel sound: /ĭ/

Revise the sounds of two letter blends:

/fi/, /hi/, /ki/, /li/, /pi/, /si/

Teach word building with final /t/.

High-Frequency Words	Picture Noun	Generative Sight Words
not all were	candle	Friday

Ben likes to keep fit.

Ken hit the ball.

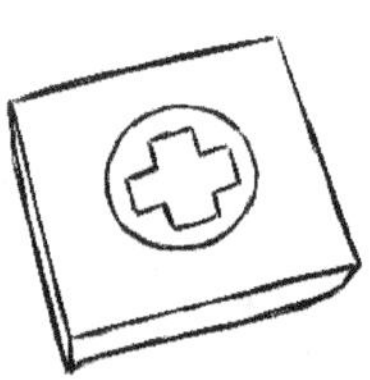

This is a little kit.

Sam likes to sit and read.

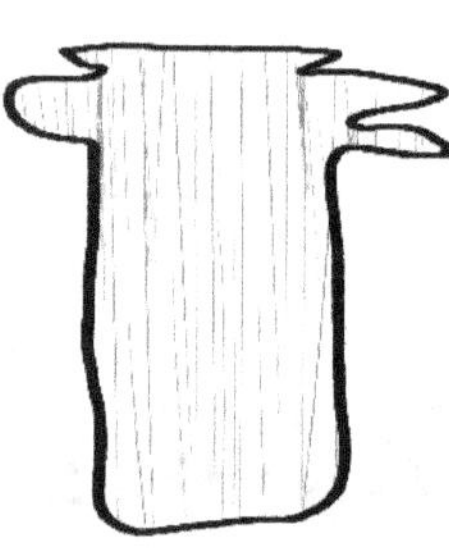

The men were in the pit.

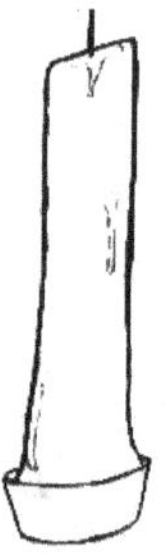

I lit the candle on Friday.
I lit it for Pam.

Hit and It

It

The bag is big.

It is big.

It is a big bag for Sam.

The van is big.

It is a big van.

It is a big bag for Sam.

Hit

Dad can hit the ball.

I can hit the ball school.

Can you hit a ball?

Keep Fit

Pat can keep fit.

Pam and Sam like to keep fit.

Dad and Dan can keep fit.

They can keep fit.

They run, jump and play!

Mell and Nell run with Dad and Dan.

Ted likes to keep fit on Friday.

Ben, Jen, and Ken walk with the dog Max.

On Friday, all the boys ran to keep fit.

They were not sad.

I ran to keep fit with the boys.

Easy Reader Level B

Speed Drill

Read these words many times. Have someone time you. See how many words you can read in a minute.

set	jet	well	pet	wet
dad	yet	wed	pat	wag
lap	Ted	tag	nap	van
bell	sell	sad	fell	tell
vet	sat	Pat	let	tap
ten	rag	net	fed	red
fit	peg	Nell	lit	pit
had	Mell	map	rat	men
can	mad	man	lad	mat
bag	hit	led	pen	hen
Ned	beg	kit	Meg	

1st Reading: _______ words in a minute

2nd Reading: _______ words in a minute

3rd Reading: _______ words in a minute

Speed Drill

Read these words many times. Have someone time you. See how many words you can read in a minute.

A	in	help	I	here
and	Friday	keep	candle	to
ball	play	all	Wednesday	tree
book	a	pretty	this	be
from	were	by	Sunday	work
game	can	one	see	want
little	Monday	woman	look	is
run	walk	words	house	jump
Thursday	like	boy	he	you
toy	have	read	girl	not
was	funny	dog	big	the
or	man			

1st Reading: _______ words in a minute

2nd Reading: _______ words in a minute

3rd Reading: _______ words in a minute

Easy Reader Level B

Three Letter Blends

Revise short vowel sound: /ĭ/

Revise the sounds of two letter blends:

/bi/, /fi/, /ni/, /pi/, /ti/, /wi/

Teach word building with final /n/.

b + i + n = bin

f + i + n = fin

p + i + n = pin

t + i + n = tin

w + i + n = win

High-Frequency Words	Picture Noun	Generative Sight Words
what we when your	fish	Saturday school

Sentences with -in words

What is in the big bin?

We can see the pan in the big bin.

When can you get the big pin?

The fish has a little fin.

Don can win on Saturday.

Your kit is in the tin at school.

In **and** Inn

They are in the jet.

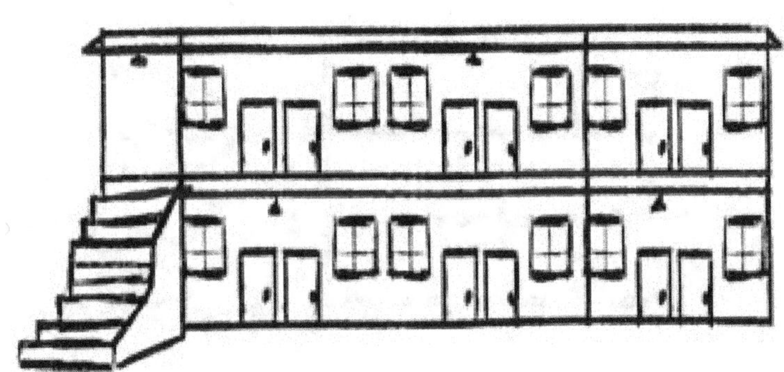

Nell is at the inn with dad.

Days

Sunday and Saturday, I am at the pretty house.

Monday, Tuesday and Wednesday I can play at school.

Thursday and Friday, I read at school.

I can read big and little books at school you see.

I want you to read and play with Nell and Ken.

Easy Reader Level B

Speed Drill

Read these words many times. Have someone time you. See how many words you can read in a minute.

bag	rag	tag	pen	hen
bell	sell	well	fell	tell
can	fan	sad	lad	mat
dad	cat	Pat	pat	wag
fit	hit	kit	lit	pit
had	sat	bat	rat	men
lap	cap	map	nap	van
leg	peg	egg	Meg	beg
Ned	Ted	wed	hat	bad
ran	mad	fat	pan	wet
rap	wrap	man	pet	tin
set	jet	net	pin	red
sit	bin	fin	fed	tap
ten	bed	led	let	Nell
vet	yet	get	yell	Mell
win				

1st Reading: _______ words in a minute

2nd Reading: _______ words in a minute

3rd Reading: _______ words in a minute

Speed Drill

Read these words many times. Have someone time you. See how many words you can read in a minute.

game	can	one	Wednesday	tree
from	were	by	this	be
book	a	pretty	Sunday	work
ball	play	all	see	want
and	Friday	keep	look	is
A	in	help	I	here
little	Monday	woman	house	jump
run	walk	words	he	you
what	were	your	when	fish
was	funny	dog	big	the
toy	have	read	girl	not
Thursday	like	boy	candle	to
or	man	Saturday	school	

1st Reading: _______ words in a minute

2nd Reading: _______ words in a minute

3rd Reading: _______ words in a minute

Three Letter Blends

Revise short vowel sound: /ĭ/
Revise the sounds of two letter blends:

/bi/, /fi/, /gi/, /hi/, /ji/, /pi/, /wi/

Teach word building with final /g/.

b + i + g = big 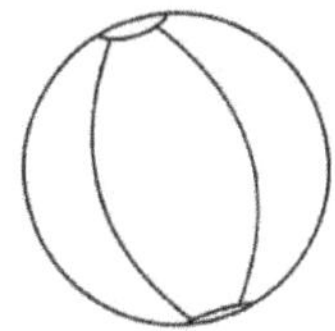   d + i + g = dig 

f + i + g = fig    g + i + g = gig 

p + i + g = pig    w + i + g = wig 

j + i + g = jig 

Colour Words

blue	black	brown	green	orange
pink	purple	red	white	yellow

Sentences with -ig words

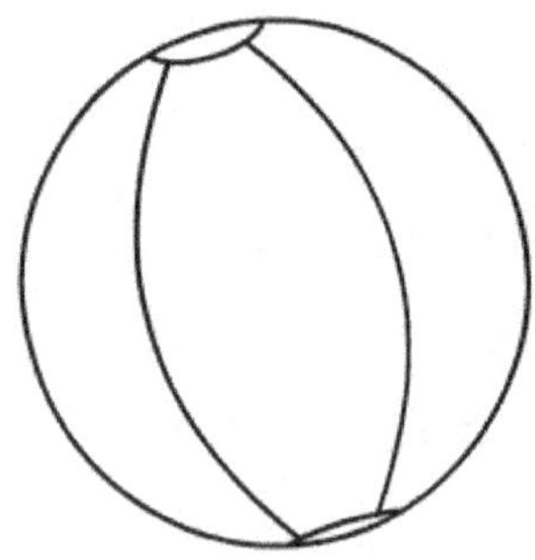

We can play with the big blue ball.

Here is a black wig for Pat.

I like to eat fig with Mell and Nell.

I want to get a brown gig for Pam.

They can do the jig.

Ken helps to dig the pit for Dad.

The white pig wants to play with the dog, Max.

Easy Reader Level B

Colours at a House

Look at a green bat at the house.

Yellow and blue is the mat, on it I sat.

Here is a bed.

It is a little red bed.

Look at the big, brown pig.

The big, brown pig is in a white pen.

Black and orange is the colour of the van.

Look at Pam with a pink, pretty fan for Dad.

Is your house purple?

Win

A little, red and black fin.

A big, green tin.

A pretty, brown and blue bin.

A little white pin.

In a yellow and blue house, on an orange bed!

I want to win the fin, bin, pin and bin on Saturday!

Easy Reader Level B

Speed Drill

Read these words many times. Have someone time you. See how many words you can read in a minute.

ten	bed	led	fed	red
bell	sell	well	fell	tell
gig	big	dig	fig	pig
ran	mad	fat	hat	Nell
can	fan	sad	lad	mat
vet	yet	get	let	tap
fit	hit	kit	lit	pit
Ned	Ted	wed	Meg	beg
lap	cap	map	nap	van
rap	wrap	man	pan	bad
dad	cat	Pat	pat	wag
bag	rag	tag	pen	hen
set	jet	net	pet	wet
sit	bin	fin	pin	tin
had	sat	bat	rat	men
jig	wig	win	peg	egg
leg	yell	Mell		

1ˢᵗ Reading: _______ words in a minute2ⁿᵈ Reading: _______ words in a minute

3ʳᵈ Reading: _______ words in a minute

Speed Drill

Read these words many times. Have someone time you. See how many words you can read in a minute.

blue	black	brown	house	jump
book	a	pretty	Sunday	work
from	were	by	this	be
game	can	one	Wednesday	tree
ball	play	all	see	want
and	Friday	keep	look	is
A	in	help	I	here
little	Monday	woman	white	the
or	man	Saturday	when	fish
pink	purple	red	school	orange
run	walk	words	he	you
Thursday	like	boy	green	yellow
toy	have	read	girl	not
was	funny	dog	candle	to
what	were	your	big	

1st Reading: _______ words in a minute

2nd Reading: _______ words in a minute

3rd Reading: _______ words in a minute

Easy Reader Level B

Three Letter Blends

Revise short vowel sound: /ĭ /

Revise the sounds of two letter blends:

/hi/, /ki/, /li/, /ri/

Teach word building with final /d/.

h + i + d = hid

l + i + d = lid

k + i + d = kid

r + i + d = rid

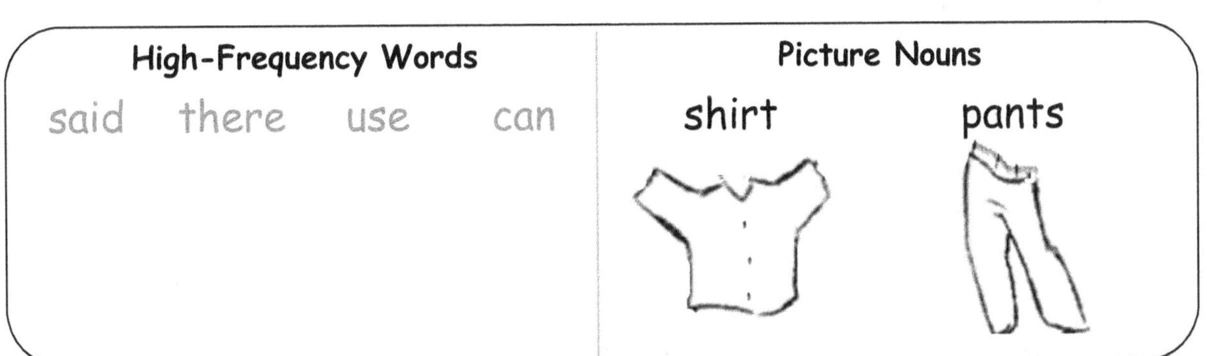

High-Frequency Words	Picture Nouns
said there use can	shirt pants

Sentences with -id words

There is the lid for the bin.

The little kid is funny.

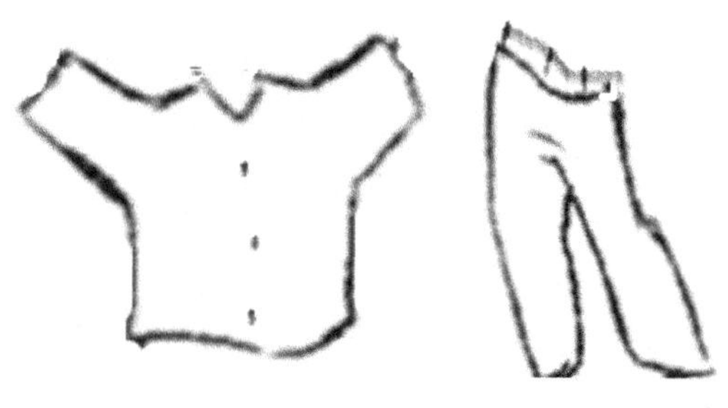

He hid the shirt and pants from his dad.

Pam hid from dad.

Dad said to get rid of toy with the mess. You can use the bin in the pen.

Easy Reader Level B

Speed Drill

Read these words many times. Have someone time you. See how many words you can read in a minute.

fit	hit	kit	pet	wet
gig	big	dig	pat	wag
jig	wig	rid	nap	van
dad	cat	Pat	pin	tin
set	jet	net	fell	tell
leg	peg	egg	let	tap
sit	bin	fin	fed	red
lap	cap	map	lit	pit
rap	wrap	man	fig	pig
can	fan	sad	rat	men
Ned	Ted	wed	lad	mat
bag	rag	tag	pen	hen
kid	lid	hid	Meg	beg
had	sat	bat	pan	bad
ran	mad	fat	hat	Mell
bell	sell	well	yell	win
ten	bed	led	Nell	get
vet	yet			

1st Reading: _______ words in a minute 2nd Reading: _______ words in a minute

3rd Reading: _______ words in a minute

Speed Drill

Read these words many times. Have someone time you. See how many words you can read in a minute.

what	were	your	big	to
were	be	from	this	by
was	funny	dog	candle	pants
toy	have	read	girl	not
Thursday	like	boy	green	yellow
said	there	use	candle	shirt
run	walk	words	he	you
play	want	ball	see	all
pink	purple	red	school	orange
Monday	the	little	white	woman
man	fish	or	when	Saturday
in	here	A	I	help
Friday	is	and	look	keep
can	tree	game	Wednesday	one
black	jump	blue	house	brown
a	work	book	Sunday	pretty

1st Reading: _______ words in a minute

2nd Reading: _______ words in a minute

3rd Reading: _______ words in a minute

Easy Reader Level B

Three Letter Blends

Revise short vowel sound: /ĭ/

Revise the sounds of two letter blends:

/fi/, /mi/, /si/

Teach word building with final /x/.

High-Frequency Words	Picture Noun	Generative Sight Words
each which she an	chair	mother father

Sentences with -ix words

Dad can fix the chair for Sam.

She can mix the egg in the pan.

Each pan had six pants.

Which shirt is in the van?

There is an ant on the chair.

Easy Reader Level B

Mother and Father

This is mother.

Mother is a woman.

She is big.

That is father.

Father is a man.

He is big.

My father and mother play with me.

We keep fit on a Monday.

Each day we read big books.

They help me to read big and little words.

They want me to read books at school to help boys and girls.

Speed Drill

Read these words many times. Have someone time you. See how many words you can read in a minute.

vet	yet	get	let	tap
ten	bed	led	fed	red
sit	mat	fin	pin	tin
set	jet	net	pet	wet
rap	wrap	man	pan	bad
ran	mad	fat	hat	lad
Ned	Ted	wed	Meg	beg
lap	cap	map	nap	van
kid	lid	hid	rid	leg
jig	wig	yell	Mell	Nell
had	sat	bat	rat	men
gig	big	dig	fig	pig
fix	mix	six	peg	egg
fit	hit	kit	lit	pit
dad	cat	Pat	pat	wag
can	fan	sad	fell	tell
bell	sell	well	pen	hen
bag	rag	win	bin	tag

1st Reading: _______ words in a minute2nd Reading: _______ words in a minute

3rd Reading: _______ words in a minute

Easy Reader Level B

Speed Drill

Read these words many times. Have someone time you. See how many words you can read in a minute.

run	walk	words	he	you
said	there	use	candle	shirt
what	were	your	big	to
Thursday	like	boy	green	yellow
toy	have	read	girl	not
was	funny	dog	candle	pants
were	be	from	this	by
play	want	ball	see	all
pink	purple	red	school	orange
Monday	the	little	white	woman
mother	father	or	when	Saturday
man	fish	A	I	help
in	here	and	look	keep
Friday	is	she	an	chair
each	which	game	Wednesday	one
can	tree	blue	house	brown
black	jump	book	Sunday	pretty
a	work			

1st Reading: _______ words in a minute 2nd Reading: _______ words in a minute 3rd Reading: _______ words in a minute

Twin Consonant Ending

Revise short vowel sound: /ĭ/

Revise the sounds of two letter blends:

/bi/, /fi/, /gi/, /hi/, /ji/, /mi/, /wi/

Teach word building with final /ll/.

b + i + ll = bill

i + ll = ill

B + i + ll = Bill

f + i + ll = fill

h + i + ll = hill

m + i + ll = mill

J + i + ll = Jill

High-Frequency Words	Picture Nouns	Generative Sight Words
how their if will do	bicycle	ride

Sentences with –ill words

I will get the bill for dad.

The mill is by the hill.

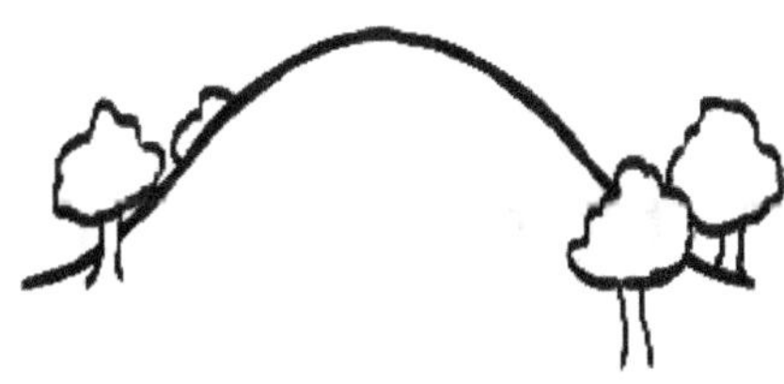

I want to walk to the hill with Jill.

Bill is ill. How will he get well?

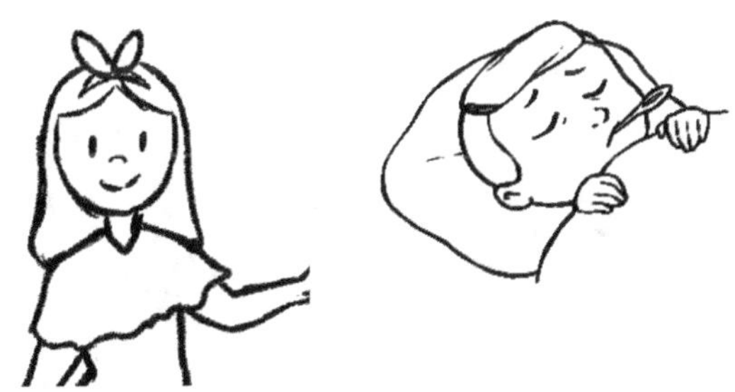

What if Jill and Bill do not come to school on Friday?

Jill is by the well. She will fill the pan for me.

The Hill

How will I get to the hill?

I will ride a bicycle to the hill.

Jill and Bill will be there by the hill.

They will be at the hill with a bill in the till.

The pan I will fill and play on the hill.

They will get their dog and a cat to play on the hill.

If their dog will not play on the hill,

I will get their cat to play on the hill.

Jill and Ben are not ill to play on the hill.

We are not sad as we play on the hill.

Easy Reader Level B

There and Their

There is a big hill. You can ride your bicycle there.

Their hands are wet.

Their house is big and pretty.

Speed Drill

Read these words many times. Have someone time you. See how many words you can read in a minute.

yell	Mell	tag	rat	men
vet	yet	fin	Bill	hill
ten	bed	Nell	fed	red
sit	bin	well	fell	tell
set	jet	fill	fig	pig
rap	wrap	hid	hat	win
ran	mad	led	Jill	mat
Ned	Ted	net	lad	tap
leg	peg	Pat	let	pit
lap	cap	get	lit	beg
kid	lid	egg	Meg	van
jig	wig	fat	nap	bad
ill	bill	dig	pan	wag
had	sat	map	pat	hen
gig	big	bat	pen	wet
fix	mix	six	pet	tin
fit	hit	wed	pin	bag
dad	cat	man	rag	mill

Easy Reader Level B

Speed Drill

Read these words many times. Have someone time you. See how
many words you can read in a minute.

can	fan	kit	sell	sad
bell				

1st Reading: _______ words in a minute

2nd Reading: _______ words in a minute

3rd Reading: _______ words in a minute

Speed Drill

Read these words many times. Have someone time you. See how many words you
can read in a minute.

said	there	use	candle	shirt
Thursday	like	boy	green	yellow
toy	have	read	girl	not
was	funny	dog	candle	pants
were	be	from	this	by
what	were	your	big	to
run	walk	words	he	you
play	want	ball	see	all
pink	purple	red	school	work
Monday	the	little	white	woman

Speed Drill

Read these words many times. Have someone time you. See how many words you can read in a minute.

mother	father	or	when	Saturday
man	fish	A	I	help
in	here	and	look	keep
Friday	is	she	an	chair
each	which	blue	house	brown
do	how	book	Sunday	pretty
can	tree	game	Wednesday	one
black	jump	their	if	will
bicycle	ride	a		

1st Reading: _______ words in a minute

2nd Reading: _______ words in a minute

3rd Reading: _______ words in a minute

Easy Reader Level B

Three Letter Blends

Revise short vowel sound: /ĭ /

Revise the sounds of two letter blends:

/di/, /hi/, /pi/, /si/, /ti/

Teach word building with final /p/.

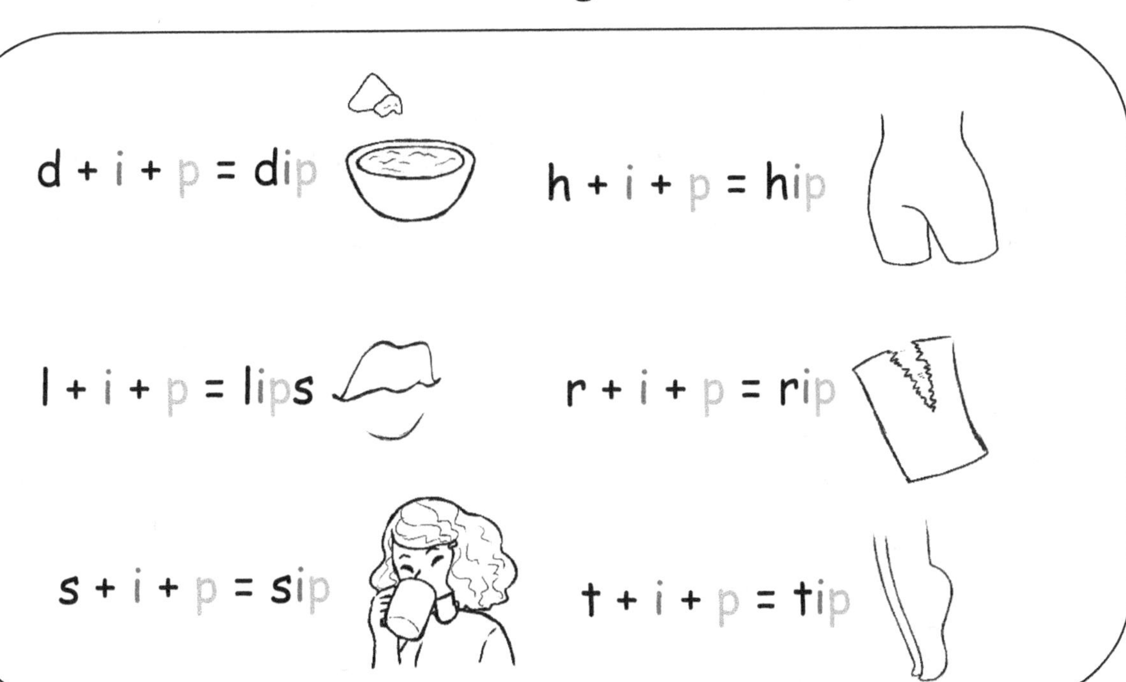

High-Frequency Words				Picture Noun
up	other	about	out	shoes

Sentences with -ip words

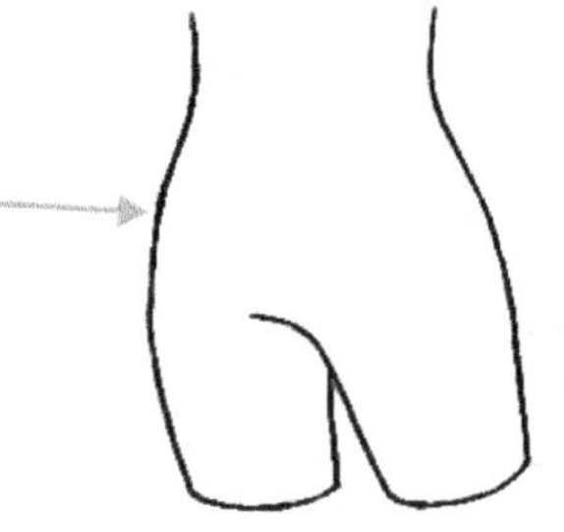

Put you hand on your hip
and do the jig.

"What big lips you have,"
said the boy.

Did you rip the book?

Get the pet out of the
house!

Tell dad about the wet
shoes.

They had the other boy
in the house.

Easy Reader Level B

Tip

The tip of the pen is little.

Tim can tip and the woman can sip.

The man gets a tip when he works for me.

Nell can tip the dip.

The Pig

The dog and the cat walk up the other hill.

The big pig ran out of the house and up the hill.

The dog and the cat sat on the pig on the big hill.

The pig is about to pat the dog on the big hill.

The pig ran up the hill with the fig in the wig.

Dad and I

Here I am.

There is Dad.

We want to play up the hill.

My dad and I go up the hill. He likes to run and play with the hen.

I will not run up the hill, I will ride a bicycle.

That is what Dad and I do on Saturdays.

Do you want to play with Dad and I?

Speed Drill

Read these words many times. Have someone time you. See how many words you can read in a minute.

had	sat	bat	rat	men
gig	big	dig	fig	pig
leg	peg	egg	win	tell
ran	mad	fat	hat	fell
ill	bill	fill	Bill	hill
sit	bin	fix	mix	tap
vet	yet	get	let	tip
kid	lid	hid	rid	fin
fit	hit	kit	pin	red
ten	bed	led	fed	sip
dip	hip	lips	rip	bad
rap	wrap	man	pan	van
lap	cap	map	nap	six
jig	wig	mill	Jill	tin
yell	Mell	Nell	lit	wet
set	jet	net	pet	wag
dad	cat	Pat	pat	mat

Easy Reader Level B

Speed Drill

Read these words many times. Have someone time you. See how many words you can read in a minute.

can	fan	sad	lad	hen
bag	rag	tag	pen	beg
Ned	Ted	wed	Meg	pit
bell	sell	well		

1st Reading: _______ words in a minute

2nd Reading: _______ words in a minute

3rd Reading: _______ words in a minute

Speed Drill

Read these words many times. Have someone time you. See how many words you can read in a minute.

what	were	your	big	to
were	be	from	this	by
was	funny	dog	candle	pants
toy	have	read	girl	not
mother	father	or	when	Saturday
pink	purple	red	school	work
play	want	ball	see	all
run	walk	words	he	you

Speed Drill

Read these words many times. Have someone time you. See how many words you can read in a minute.

said	there	use	candle	shirt
Thursday	like	boy	green	yellow
up	other	about	out	shoes
Monday	the	little	white	woman
man	fish	A	I	help
in	here	and	look	keep
Friday	is	she	an	chair
each	which	blue	house	brown
do	how	book	Sunday	pretty
can	tree	game	Wednesday	one
black	jump	their	if	will
bicycle	ride	a		

1st Reading: _________ words in a minute

2nd Reading: _________ words in a minute

3rd Reading: _________ words in a minute

Easy Reader Level B

Phonetic Words Assessment 3

Name: ___________________   Date: _______________

Read the words.

_fix	_mix	_six	_ten	_sat
_fed	_bat	_tin	_vet	_fill
_fan	_lap	_well	_wet	_hat
_dig	_big	_win	_yet	_lad
_cap	_yell	_lips	_sip	_let
_egg	_Pam	_tip	_rip	_lit
_dip	_hip	_bad	_bag	_mad
_get	_bell	_cat	_bed	_man
_wag	_bill	_fat	_Bill	_set
_van	_dad	_pin	_bin	_kid
_fin	_ham	_sit	_wig	_hill
_tap	_fit	_fig	_gig	_pit
_tag	_jet	_wed	_beg	_rat
_sell	_fell	_red	_Pat	_Meg

Phonetic Words Assessment 3

Name: _________________   Date: _____________

Read the words.

_tell	_jam	_net	_pig	_mat
_Jill	_jig	_mill	_Ted	_Mell
_leg	_led	_Nell	_nap	_rag
_kit	_hit	_pat	_Ned	_sad
_ill	_pan	_peg	_can	_rap
_hid	_lid	_pet	_pen	_rid
_hen	_had	_map		

Score

____

104

93-104 words correct: **Excellent**
78-92 words correct: **Satisfactory**
52-77 words correct: **Needs Improvement**
1-51 words correct: **Re-teach the unit**

High Frequency Words Assessment 3

Name: _______________________   Date: _______________

Read the words.

_we	_when	_your	_can	_said
_but	_not	_what	_all	_were
_will	_up	_other	_about	_out
_she	_do	_how	_their	_if
_there	_use	_an	_each	_which
_a	_it	_with	_this	_by
_in	_was	_they	_from	_on
_to	_he	_his	_have	_words
_the	_is	_for	_I	_or
_and	_that	_as	_be	_had
_of	_you	_are	_at	_one

Score

_____

55

50-55 words correct: **Excellent**

41-49 words correct: **Satisfactory**

28-40 words correct: **Needs Improvement**

1-29 words correct: **Re-teach the unit**

Unit 3 Short Vowel /O/
Three Letter Blends

Revise short vowel sound: /ŏ/

Revise the sounds of two letter blends:

/co/, /do/, /po/, /ro/, /lo/, /go/

Teach word building with final /t/.

c + o + t = cot

d + o + t = dot

p + o + t = pot

r + o + t = rot

l + o + t = lot

g + o + t = got

High-Frequency Words	Picture Noun	Generative Sight Words
many then them these so	water	funny

Sentences with –ot words

This little cot is for me.

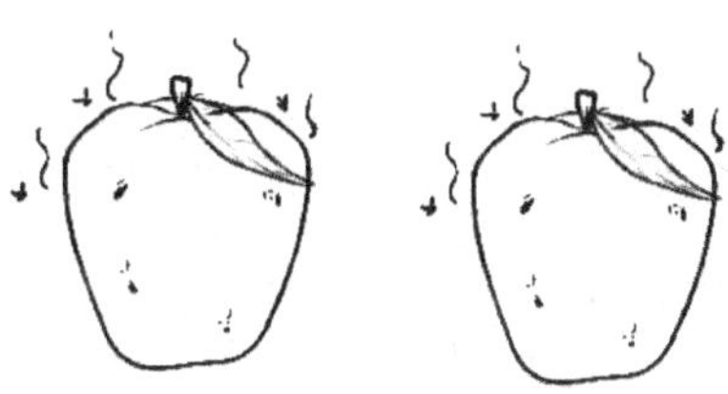

There is a big dot.

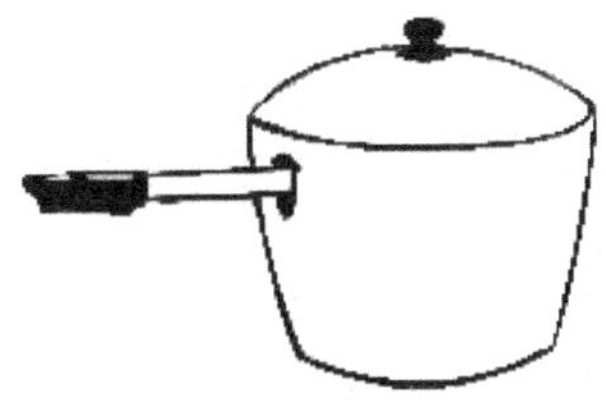

Is there water in the pot?

These will rot.

There are vans in the lot. How many of them do you see?

I got these vans from the lot.

The Cat with the Dot

The little cat has a dot.
The little cat with the dot sat on the cot.

The little cat got so hot that he was sad.

"There is water in a pan." said Tom to them. They look
for the many mats by the tub. Tom then let the cat
to sit in the pan of water.

The little cat with the dot looks at them.
The little cat with the dot sat in the pan of water.
I like the little cat with the dot.

These

That is your shirt but

These are his pants.

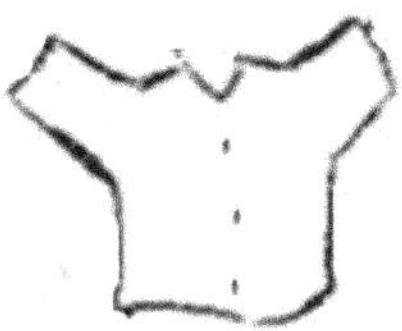

That is your rag but

These are his shoes.

That is the chair, on it you sit and

These are the books that I will read with you.

Tell them of the many books we have.

So many funny books to read!

These are books you can read!

Speed Drill

Read these words many times. Have someone time you. See how many words you can read in a minute.

yell	Mell	Nell	rag	tag
vet	yet	get	let	tap
tip	cot	dot	pot	rot
ten	bed	led	fed	red
sit	bin	fin	pin	tin
set	jet	net	pet	wet
rap	tell	man	pan	bad
ran	mad	fat	hat	beg
Ned	Ted	wed	Meg	bag
leg	peg	egg	win	van
lap	cap	map	nap	lot
kid	lid	hid	rid	got
jig	wig	mill	Jill	hill
ill	bill	fill	Bill	men
had	sat	bat	rat	pig
gig	big	dig	fig	hen
fix	mix	six	pen	pit
fit	hit	kit	lit	sip
dip	hip	lips	rip	fell

Easy Reader Level B

Speed Drill

Read these words many times. Have someone time you. See how many words you can read in a minute.

dad	cat	Pat	pat	wag
can	fan	sad	lad	mat
bell	sell	well		

1st Reading: _______ words in a minute

2nd Reading: _______ words in a minute

3rd Reading: _______ words in a minute

Speed Drill

Read these words many times. Have someone time you. See how many words you can read in a minute.

all	play	want	ball	see
bicycle	ride	a	work	will
black	jump	their	if	water
can	tree	game	Wednesday	one
chair	you	is	she	an
do	how	book	Sunday	pretty
each	which	blue	house	brown

Speed Drill

Read these words many times. Have someone time you. See how many words you can read in a minute.

funny	man	fish	A	I
help	in	here	and	look
keep	then	them	these	so
many	father	or	when	Saturday
mother	pink	purple	red	school
he	said	there	use	candle
shirt	up	other	about	out
shoes	have	read	girl	not
toy	funny	dog	candle	pants
was	be	from	this	by
were	were	your	big	to
what	Monday	the	little	white
woman	Thursday	like	boy	green
yellow	run	walk	words	

1st Reading: _______ words in a minute

2nd Reading: _______ words in a minute

3rd Reading: _______ words in a minute

Easy Reader Level B

Three Letter Blends

Revise short vowel sound: /ŏ/

Revise the sounds of two letter blends:

/fŏ/, /gŏ/, /hŏ/, /jŏ/, /lŏ/

Teach word building with final /g/.

f + o + g = fog

h + o + g = hog

j + o + g = jog

l + o + g = log

High-Frequency Words	Generative Sight Words
some her would make like	friends

The Hogs in the Fog

A pig is a hog and a hog is a pig!

That is so said the woman in the van.

She sells hogs to the men at the inn.

They will use the hogs to make ham.

Some of her friends do not like to eat them.

Look at the fog on the hill!

The truck with the hogs is in the fog. There are many

hogs in the van.

The woman had all her hogs in the van.

They sat on the log in the van. Max the dog was

there with them.

Easy Reader Level B

The woman would have to sell all the hogs at the inn.

Then it would be her and Max, her dog in the fog.

She got in her van with her dog and the hogs in the

fog.

Three Letter Blends

Revise short vowel sound: /ŏ/

Revise the sounds of two letter blends:

/hŏ/, /mŏ/, /tŏ/

Teach word building with final /p/.

h + o + p = hop

m + o + p = mop

t + o + p = top

High-Frequency Words

nine	six	two	five	four
seven	three	eight		

Hop to the Top

Use the mop and hop to the top with Don.

Jump five hops and jump to the top.

Do seven hops and run up the hill.

Use a mop and do one hop.

Jump eight hops and you will see,

Dad, Pam and Sam at the top.

Tell them to jump nine hops and do a jig.

Then run to the other hill and jump six hops.

Two, nine, three, and four, these are the hops to win

at the top!

Three Letter Blends

Revise short vowel sound: /ŏ/

Revise the sounds of two letter blends:

/cŏ/, /dŏ/, /gŏ/, /lŏ/, /pŏ/, /rŏ/

Teach word building with final /x/.

b + o + x = box

o + x = ox

c + o + x = cox

f + o + x = fox

High-Frequency Words

him   into   time   has   more   two   look

Easy Reader Level B

The Fox and the Box

Cox had a funny ox at his house.

The ox has more than two pet friends.

One of his friends is a fox.

Cox likes the fox.

To him, the fox is funny.

Cox and the vet have a box for the ox and the fox.

The box is in the pen.

The fox jumps into the pen.

The fox and the ox see the box.

Cox and his friend want to look at what the ox and

the fox would do.

The ox has more time to look at the big, pretty box.

The fox ran into the pen.

They look at the pink box.

The fox and the ox play and jump into the pink box.

Cox and the vet had put a fox in the box to be their friend.

Easy Reader Level B

Speed Drill

Read these words many times. Have someone time you. See how many words you can read in a minute.

dip	hip	lips	rip	sip
log	fog	hog	jog	six
tip	cot	dot	pot	rot
gig	big	dig	fig	pig
ill	bill	fill	Bill	hill
kid	lid	hid	rid	lot
jig	wig	mill	Jill	got
set	jet	net	pet	wet
vet	yet	get	let	tap
lap	cap	map	nap	van
rap	wrap	man	pan	bad
can	fan	sad	lad	mat
ran	mad	fat	hat	wag
dad	cat	Pat	pat	men
had	sat	bat	rat	hen
bag	rag	tag	pen	red
ten	bed	led	fed	beg
Ned	Ted	wed	Meg	tell

Speed Drill

Read these words many times. Have someone time you. See how many words you can read in a minute.

leg	peg	egg	fell	ox
bell	sell	well	box	pit
yell	Mell	Nell	lit	tin
fit	hit	kit	pin	hog
sit	bin	fin	fog	lot
win	got	log	rot	jog
cot	dot	pot	fox	mix
hop	mop	top	fix	

1st Reading: _______ words in a minute

2nd Reading: _______ words in a minute

3rd Reading: _______ words in a minute

Easy Reader Level B

Speed Drill

Read these words many times. Have someone time you. See how many words you can read in a minute.

do	how	book	Sunday	pretty
chair	you	is	she	an
can	tree	game	Wednesday	one
black	jump	their	if	water
bicycle	ride	a	work	will
all	play	want	ball	see
mother	pink	purple	red	school
many	father	or	when	Saturday
keep	then	them	these	so
help	in	here	and	look
funny	man	fish	A	I
each	which	blue	house	brown
words	said	there	use	candle
shirt	up	other	about	out
woman	Thursday	like	boy	green
what	Monday	the	little	white
were	were	your	big	to
was	be	from	this	by

Speed Drill

Read these words many times. Have someone time you. See how many words you
can read in a minute.

toy	funny	dog	candle	pants
four	seven	three	eight	him
friends	nine	six	two	five
into	time	has	more	not
shoes	have	read	girl	like
some	her	would	make	he
yellow	run	walk		

1st Reading: _______ words in a minute

2nd Reading: _______ words in a minute

3rd Reading: _______ words in a minute

Easy Reader Level B

Phonetic Words Assessment 4

Name: _________________________   Date: _______________

Read the words.

_wag	_bill	_cat	_Bill	_kit
_van	_dad	_fat	_bin	_jog
_tell	_jam	_net	_man	_Jill
_Ted	_Mell	_mat	_kid	_ill
_tap	_fit	_rat	_lad	_hid
_tag	_jet	_fig	_sat	_hen
_sit	_gig	_pit	_let	_had
_sell	_egg	_wed	_fill	_hit
_map	_ran	_men	_Meg	_hop
_leg	_led	_Nell	_nap	_jig
_pat	_Ned	_mop	_top	_set
_pan	_peg	_Pat	_mill	_rag
_lid	_pet	_can	_rap	_sad

Phonetic Words Assessment 4

Name: _____________________   Date: _______________

Read the words.

_pen	_rid	_lot	_bad	_bed
_got	_log	_fog	_hog	_rip
_get	_bell	_fix	_mix	_lit
_fox	_box	_ox	_six	_ten
_fin	_ham	_pin	_fed	_bat
_tin	_vet	_fan	_lap	_well
_wet	_dip	_hip	_tip	_bag
_dig	_big	_win	_yet	_rot
_cot	_dot	_pot	_cap	_yell
_wrap	_sip	_beg	_fell	_red
_lips	_hat	_Pam	_lips	_hat

Score

_____

120

108-120 words correct: **Excellent**

90-107 words correct: **Satisfactory**

60-89 words correct: **Needs Improvement**

1-59 words correct: **Re-teach the unit**

Easy Reader Level B

High Frequency Words Assessment 4

Name: ________________________   Date: ________________

Read each word.

_will	_up	_other	_about	_out
_we	_when	_your	_can	_said
_there	_use	_an	_each	which
_she	_do	_how	_their	_if
_but	_not	_what	_all	_were
_some	_her	_would	_make	_like
_many	_then	_them	_these	_so
_him	_into	_time	_has	_look
_to	_he	_his	_have	_words
_the	_is	_for	_I	_or
_of	_you	_are	_at	_one
_in	_was	_they	_from	_on
_and	_that	_as	_be	_had

High Frequency Words Assessment 4

Name: ___________________   Date: _______________

Read each word.

_a	_it	_with	_this	_by
_two	_more	_go	_see	

Score

____

72

65-72 words correct: **Excellent**
54-64 words correct: **Satisfactory**
37-53 words correct: **Needs Improvement**
1-36 words correct: **Re-teach the unit**

Three Letter Blends

Revise short vowel sound: /ŭ/

Revise the sounds of two letter blends:

/bu/, /cu/, /hu/, /nu/

Teach word building with final /t/.

c + u + t = cut 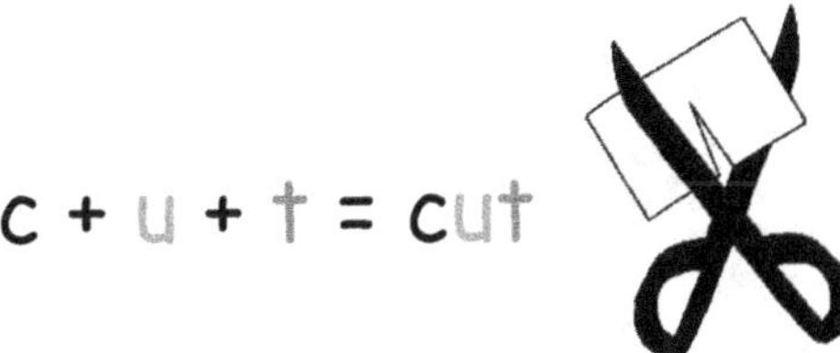   h + u + t = hut 

n + u + t = nut    b + u + t = but

High-Frequency Words

write   go   see   number   no   way   could   people

The Little Hut

There is a little hut that was blue and pink.

I can see it from the top of the hill.

It is on the way up to the hill.

There was no way that I could miss it.

A number of people would go to the hut to cut nuts.

Dad said the men could cut nuts in the hut.

On Tuesday and Thursday, the people would cut nuts
in the blue and pink hut.

I will write about the nuts in my little book.

Easy Reader Level B

If You Could

What would you do if you could walk up a big hill?

Would you tell me funny words?

Would you have a mat to sit on?

Would other people be there?

If you could walk up a big hill,

Tell what would you do?

Get Up

Get up, Nell

Get up, Mell

Get up, Dad

Get up!

Max and I want to go and play.

Pam and Sam like to play with Max.

Dad and I can run and play.

Get up Mell!

Get up Nell!

Get up Dad!

Get up!

Easy Reader Level B

Three Letter Blends

Revise short vowel sound: /ŭ/

Revise the sounds of two letter blends:

/cu/, /pu/

Teach word building with final /p/.

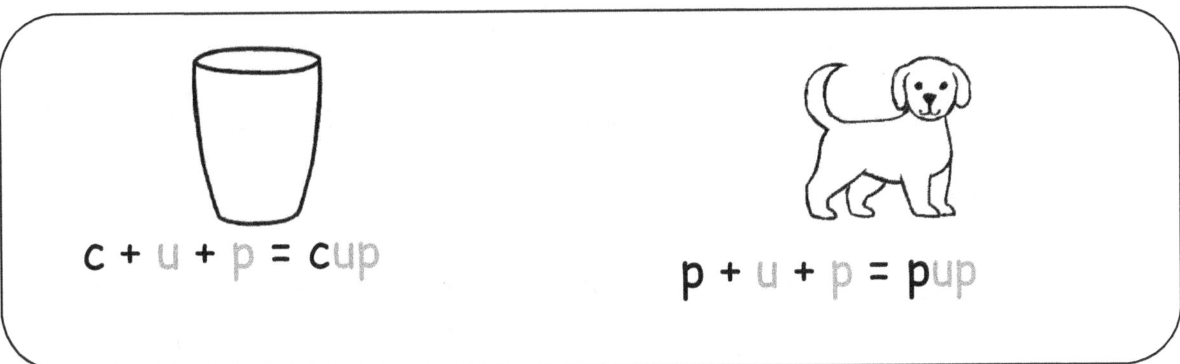

High-Frequency Words

than   first   water   been   called   who   my

A Pup

There is a little pup at my house.
It is black and white.
The pup likes to play with Mac, my dog more than
Don.

First, it would sit on my bed, and then it would run to
the pen.

I called to the pup to play with me but the pup ran to
the tub of water - there was a mess!

There was water on the mats, on the cot and on dad!
If it had not been for Pam and Sam, I would have
been mad.

Who wants this pup in their house?
This funny pup that is at my house.

Easy Reader Level B

Three Letter Blends

Revise short vowel sound: /ŭ/

Revise the sounds of two letter blends:

/bu/, /fu/, /gu/, /ru/, /nu/, /su/

Teach word building with final /n/.

b + u + n = bun   f + u + n = fun 

g + u + n = gun    r + u + n = run 

n + u + n = nun    s + u + n = sun 

High-Frequency Words

am   its   now   find   long   down

Mum and The Nun

Each day mum and the nun run for fun in the sun.

On Sunday, mum and the nun run for fun in the sun.

On Monday, mum and the nun make bun and run down a long hill for fun in the sun.

On Tuesday and Wednesday, mum and the nun call the man with the gun to find the fox, make bun and run down a long for fun in the sun.

On Thursday and Friday, mum and the nun take a tan in the sun, call the man with the gun to find the fox, make bun and run down a long for fun in the sun.

Sunday, Monday, Tuesday, Wednesday, Thursday and Friday, mum and the nun had fun in the sun.

Easy Reader Level B

Now, the man with the gun could not find the fox in the sun. He could see its den as he looks for the fox in the sun.

I am sad that the man could not find the fox in the sun.

Twin Consonant Ending

Revise short vowel sound: /ŭ/

Revise the sounds of two letter blends:

/bŭ/, /fŭ/

Teach word building with final /zz/.

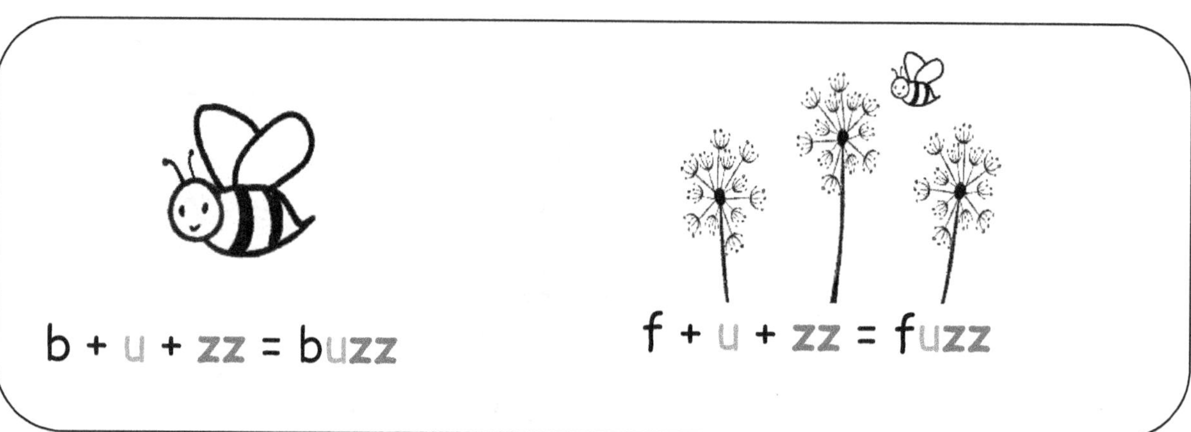

High-Frequency Words

day   did   get   come   made   may   part

Easy Reader Level B

Buzz the Bee

Buzz! Buzz! That is Buzz the bee.
He zips and zaps in the fuzz all day.

Buzz and his friends get to be part of the fun.
They come to play in the fuzz and zip and zap all day
long.

Buzz and his friends can come to my house and zip
and zap all day long.

I am going to zip and zap in the fuzz with Buzz today.
Sam and I made three zaps.

We did not see Mell to zip and zap in the fuzz with
Buzz all day.

I may write about him at school in my little book.

I may ride my bicycle and zip and zap in the fuzz with Buzz all day.

Would like to be part of the fun with Buzz and his friends?

Easy Reader Level B

Saturday

I like to play in the house on a Saturday.

Ben and Ken can come on a Saturday to run and jump.

They can jump in the pen.

Ben and Ken can jump on the bed.

On Saturday we can run, jump and play.

Get up and run.

Get up and play.

Let me get up and jump.

The Bad Rat

The fat cat and a fat bat sat. The fat bat and a fat cat sat in the van. Pat ran to tap the fat cat in the van. A fan is in the van.

You and Pam tag the bag and the rag in the van. A cap is in the bag. A bad rat sat in the bag. Dad is mad. The lad had to rap to Dad.

That rat is bad! Ned and Meg yell at the rat. They are mad at the rat. The rat fell on one of the nets

Easy Reader Level B

that were in the pen. It was sad. I had to tap the net that the rat fell on.

Ned was with Ted. Ted ran for his hen that was in the pen. He led his hen from the pen. The vet was in the van. He had to be by the pen for the cat in the van. They can let the vet have the bad rat or they can sell this bad rat to the men by the well!

Bill had a red bin for the bad rat. The bin had big words on it. He hit the net to get rid of the bad rat but the bad rat sat in the net. What a bad rat! They were all sad.

We rip the net when the bad rat sat. Bill and Jill tip the bin. Each bin had one red lid. Can you tell your dad what the bad rat did? The bad rat ran out of the net!

It ran to the bin! The bad rat was there in the bin.

Jill said an ant was in the bin.

Bill and Jill did a rap. Their dad and the man did

about ten jigs. The other men sat and tap up by the

well.

Which vet will have this bad rat? How will the vet use

this bad rat? If she has a big lab, she can have the

bad rat. The vet got the bad rat so that is how we

got rid of the bad rat. What will the vet do with the

bad rat?

The bad rat met many other rats at the lab. These

rats were so big. The vet fed them well. Some of

them sat on top of a box but two of them would tap

on a log. The more they tap, the more the vets write

and then look at each other.

                                    Easy Reader Level B

One time, Don and I got into the lab like a cat. We had to go and see the bad rat. The bad rat was on top of her box. We make a hop. The bad rat has a box!

There were a number of people at the lab. A pup ran to Don. Don put him out of the way. We could not let the vet buzz the bell. There was no way we would get out of the lab.

That day, the lab was as hot as the sun. My lips were hot. First, we had to get some water. I called to Don who has been with the bad rat for a long time now. The bad rat had its fun on the box. I had to find him. This was more than what I had time for.

This day is now bad. I am hot and Don had to come now from the lab. I am so hot.

Who could tell that the lab would be so hot that day? I may have to part from Don. I made one more call to Don and ran from the lab down the log.

Speed Drill

Read these words many times. Have someone time you. See how many words you can read in a minute.

well	wet	bat	fox	Nell
ten	tip	yell	lit	jog
tag	bad	mix	pen	pin
six	log	fill	Jill	pot
sit	bin	yet	rip	wag
set	jet	cot	pat	let
rat	vet	fig	but	tell
rap	wrap	bed	pan	hat
ran	mad	wed	pig	lot
pot	tin	beg	fog	nap
Pat	rot	dot	win	cup
nut	red	dig	sip	got
Ned	Ted	van	Bill	rot
log	fog	top	Meg	map
leg	peg	pup	fed	fin
lap	cap	net	pet	lot
kit	hog	fat	fell	led

Speed Drill

Read these words many times. Have someone time you. See how many words you can read in a minute.

jig	wig	mill	hen	hog
ill	bill	men	hit	hill
hop	mop	Mell	hip	hid
had	sat	bun	cat	sun
gig	big	nun	hut	get
fuzz	buzz	gun	dot	fix
cut	fan	rid	jog	bag
run	ox	sell	bell	can
cot	tap	egg	pit	man
lips	dad	dip	fit	got
kid	lid	box	rag	

1st Reading: _______ words in a minute

2nd Reading: _______ words in a minute

3rd Reading: _______ words in a minute

Easy Reader Level B

Speed Drill

Read these words many times. Have someone time you. See how many words you can read in a minute.

mother	pink	purple	red	school
many	father	or	when	Saturday
keep	then	them	these	so
help	in	here	and	look
funny	man	fish	A	I
each	which	blue	house	brown
do	how	book	Sunday	pretty
chair	you	is	she	an
can	tree	game	Wednesday	one
black	jump	their	if	water
bicycle	ride	a	work	will
woman	Thursday	like	boy	green
what	Monday	the	little	white
were	were	your	big	to
was	be	from	this	by
toy	funny	dog	candle	pants
some	her	would	make	he
shoes	have	read	girl	like

Speed Drill

Read these words many times. Have someone time you. See how many words you can read in a minute.

shirt	up	other	about	out
into	time	has	more	not
friends	nine	six	two	five
yellow	run	walk	words	write
water	been	called	who	am
go	see	number	no	way
four	seven	find	long	down
may	part	get	come	made
its	now	my	than	first
day	did	three	eight	him
could	people	want	ball	see
all	play	use	candle	there
said				

1st Reading: _______ words in a minute

2nd Reading: _______ words in a minute

3rd Reading: _______ words in a minute

Easy Reader Level B

Phonetic Words Assessment 5

Name: _________________________   Date: _______________

Read the words.

_lips	_bad	_box	_rag	_hat
_tag	_big	_nun	_pen	_pin
_gig	_bill	_men	_hut	_get
_ill	_bin	_yet	_hit	_hill
_sit	_buzz	_gun	_rip	_wag
_fuzz	_cap	_net	_dot	_fix
_lap	_dad	_dip	_pet	_lot
_cot	_fan	_top	_fit	_got
_cut	_fog	_fat	_Meg	_bag
_log	_hog	_cot	_fell	_map
_kit	_jet	_mix	_pat	_led
_set	_lid	_fill	_rid	_let
_kid	_log	_wed	_Jill	_jog
_six	_mad	_hid	_pig	_pot
_ran	_mop	_Mell	_hip	_lot

Phonetic Words Assessment 5

Name: ___________________   Date: _______________

Read the words.

_hop	_ox	_sell	_bell	_can
_run	_peg	_pup	_fed	_fin
_leg	_red	_dig	_sip	_got
_nut	_sat	_bun	_cat	_sun
_had	_tap	_egg	_pit	_man
_Ned	_Ted	_van	_Bill	_rot
_pot	_tin	_beg	_fog	_nap
_ten	_tip	_yell	_lit	_jog
_rat	_vet	_fig	_but	_tell
_well	_wet	_bat	_fox	_Nell
_jig	_wig	_mill	_hen	_hog
_rap	_Pat	_bed	_pan	_cup
_rot	_dot	_win		

Score

114-127 words correct: **Excellent**

95-113 words correct: **Satisfactory**

____

63-94 words correct: **Needs Improvement**

127

1-6 words correct: **Re-teach the unit**

High Frequency Words Assessment 5

Name: _______________________   Date: _______________

Read the words.

_we	_when	_your	_can	_said
_some	_her	_would	_make	_like
_but	_not	_what	_all	_were
_than	_first	_water	_been	_called
_him	_into	_time	_has	_look
_many	_then	_them	_these	_so
_will	_up	_other	_about	_out
_come	_made	_may	_part	_find
_who	_am	_its	_now	_if
_she	_do	_how	_their	_number
_two	_more	_go	_see	_get
_long	_down	_day	_did	_my
_no	_way	_could	_people	_which
_there	_use	_an	_each	_on

High Frequency Words Assessment 5

Name: ______________________   Date: ________________

Read the words.

_a	_it	_with	_this	_by
_in	_was	_they	_from	_words
_to	_he	_his	_have	_or
_the	_is	_for	_I	_had
_and	_that	_as	_be	_one
_of	_you	_are	_at	_write

Score

____

100

90-100 words correct: **Excellent**
75-89 words correct: **Satisfactory**
50-74 words correct: **Needs Improvement**
1-49 words correct: **Re-teach the unit**

Final Assessment

Instructions: The learner will read each section independently with the supervision of a teacher.

1.

buzz	got	lad	will	yen
—	—	—	—	—

2.

mix	doll	Nan	vet	cup
—	—	—	—	—

3.

quit	rag	sell	hop	tux
—	—	—	—	—

4.

Zac	Jeff	pill	Tom	fuzz
—	—	—	—	—

Call each word for your teacher:

1.

new   most   sentence   before   also

___   ___   ___   ___   ___

2.

does   because   try   away   letters

___   ___   ___   ___   ___

3.

think   much   should   world   too

___   ___   ___   ___   ___

4.

place   asked   page   point   house

___   ___   ___   ___   ___

Easy Reader Level B

The Pot

Look at the pot.
There is water in the pot.
Ken and Jill put one egg in the pot.

The pot is big.
Dad will let the men use the pot.
What can they put in the hot pot?

My mum has a pot.
It can be called a pan.
She put ham in her pot.

36 words

Oral Reading Scoring Rubric

Instruction:
- ✓ Use the scoring rubric as a guide to administer the final assessment.
- ✓ The learner's scores should be recorded on the Final Assessment Scoring Sheet.
- ✓ If a learner pauses at a word/question, wait for **ONLY 5 seconds** then continue the assessment.

- ✓ Tick on the scoring sheet, the rate at which the learner reads this section. Speed can either be **Slow, Medium or Fast.**
- ✓ Record the score for each sub-section.

1. The learner is expected to read each phonetic word.
   1 mark for each correct response.
2. The learner is expected to read each high-frequency word.
   $\frac{1}{2}$ mark for each correct response.

Reading Passage

- ✓ The learner is expected to read the passage independently.
- ✓ Fluency - speed at which the passage is read.
- ✓ Insertion - reading word(s) that are not written in the passage.
- ✓ Omission - leaving out word(s) that are written in the passage.
- ✓ Substitution - replacing word(s) with another word that is not written in the passage.
- ✓ Repetition - saying word(s) that is written in the passage more than once.

Criteria	Scoring			
Fluency	Reads all sentences fluently with expression (5 marks)	Reads 7-9 sentences correctly with expression (4 marks)	Reads 4-6 sentences correctly with little expression (3 marks)	Reads 1-3 sentences correctly with or without expression (2 marks)
Insertion	No insertion (2 marks)	Inserts 1-3 Words (1 $\frac{1}{2}$ marks)	Inserts 4-7 Words (1 mark)	Inserts more than 7 words ($\frac{1}{2}$ mark)
Omission	No omission (2 marks)	Omits 1-3 Words (1 $\frac{1}{2}$ marks)	Omits 4-7 words (1 mark)	Omits more than 7 words ($\frac{1}{2}$ mark)
Substitution	No substitution (2 marks)	Substitutes 1-3 Words (1 $\frac{1}{2}$ marks)	Substitutes 4-7 words (1 mark)	Substitutes more than 7 words ($\frac{1}{2}$ mark)
Repetition	No repetition (2 marks)	Repeats 1-3 Words (1 $\frac{1}{2}$ marks)	Repeats 4-7 Words (1 mark)	Repeats more than 7 words ($\frac{1}{2}$ mark)

Easy Reader Level B

Oral Reading Scoring Rubric

Oral Questions
1. What is the passage about? *A pot/A big pot*
2. How many persons are in the story? *6 or more. Passage did can give the number of men.*
3. Name two persons mentioned in the story. *Ken, Jill, dad, mum (any two)*
4. What is a pot? *Something used for cooking or any other plausible answer.*
5. What do you think the men will do with the pot? *Any plausible answer.*

Final Assessment Scoring Sheet

Name: _________________________________ Date: _________________

Sections	Fluency			Score
	Slow	Medium	Fast	
1. Read each phonetic word				/20
2. Read each high-frequency word				/10
Reading Passage				
Fluency (speed at which the passage is read)				/5
Insertion (reading words that are not written)				/2
Omission (leaving out words that are written)				/2
Substitution (replacing a word with another word that is not written)				/2
Repetition (saying the same word more than once)				/2
Oral Questions				
6. What is the passage about?				/1
7. How many persons are in the story?				/1
8. Name two persons mentioned in the story.				/2
9. What is a pot?				/1
10. What do you think the men will do with the pot?				/2
Total Marks				/50

Easy Reader Level B

Lesson Plan Guide

Topic: _________________Duration: _______________ Date: ____________

Teaching Approach: 5E Model with Direct Instruction

Attainment Target: *Make sure you know the students Zone of Actual Development (ZAD) and that you are writing according to the students Zone of Proximal Development (ZPD). Check your Reading Assessment Records.*

Lesson Objective: What the students should be able to do by the end of the lesson.

Prior Knowledge Connection:

Reading Components	Questions
Phonemic Awareness:	Can they differentiate between sounds?
Phonics:	Can they match sound to letters in printed form?
Vocabulary:	What are the sight words that they already know at what grade level?
Fluency:	Can they read known letter sounds/words to the point of automaticity?
Comprehension:	Are the students understanding the association between sounds/letters and words? Can they understand and explain what they are reading?

Reading Components	Instructions for teaching
Phonemic Awareness, Fluency	Students need to call the sound(s) to the point of automaticity.
Phonics, Fluency	Students need to call/write the words to the point of automaticity.
Vocabulary, Fluency	Students need to call/spell the words to the point of automaticity.
Comprehension, Fluency	Students need to read passage and answer questions at various levels to the point of automaticity.
Phonemic Awareness, Phonics, Vocabulary, Comprehension, Fluency	Students need to read passage and answer questions at various levels to the point of automaticity. Provide individual instructions for students who may struggle in a group setting.

Easy Reader Level B

Procedure:

Reading Component: Phonemic Awareness, Fluency

Teaching Sequence:	Engage	
Aim:	*Revise taught sounds orally *Present new sounds and words orally	
I Do Teacher shows how it's done	**We Do** Teacher and students do it together	**You Do** Students show the teacher how it's done
Model sound(s) for students Present material in small steps. Ask questions to keep students engaged.	Teacher and students call the sounds and words together.	Students call sounds and words when prompted by the teacher.

Reading Component: Phonics, Fluency

Teaching Sequence:	Explore	
Aim:	*Revise taught sounds and words by showing letter representations *Present new sounds and words by showing them on letter representation	
I Do Teacher shows how it's done	**We Do** Teacher and students do it together	**You Do** Students show the teacher how it's done
Use different modalities to demonstrate letter – sound relationship auditory, visual or kinaesthetic	Teacher and students say sounds and words from visual representation of letter representation. Brain imprint association: write letter-sound representation in air, on paper, in sand etc.	Students make letter-sound representation when prompted by the teacher. Brain imprint association: write letter-sound representation in air, on paper, in sand etc. Play games associate with

Easy Reader Level B

Teaching Sequence:	Explore	
	Play games associate with letters Use technological devices to reinforce letter sound.	letters. Use technology e.g. video to identify letter and sound.

Reading Component: Vocabulary, Fluency

Teaching Sequence:	Explanation	
Aim:	*Learn High-Frequency words	
I Do Teacher shows how it's done	**We Do** Teacher and students do it together	**You Do** Students show the teacher how it's done
Introduce new word(s) Use different modalities/strategies to demonstrate meaning/application of word - auditory, visual or kinaesthetic	Teacher and students call/spell new word(s) Brain imprint association: word(s) representation in air, on paper, in sand, tile etc. Use words to play games Use technological devices to reinforce new words.	Students call/spell word(s) independently Brain imprint association: word(s) representation in air, on paper, in sand, tile etc. Use words to play games Use technology e.g. video to identify new words.

Reading Component: Comprehension, Fluency

Teaching Sequence:	Extension	
Aim:	*Apply phonetic and high-frequency words to reading	
I Do Teacher shows how it's done	**We Do** Teacher and students do it together	**You Do** Students show the teacher how it's done
Introduce Reading Passage with phonetic and high frequency	Teacher and students read passage together Teacher and students	Student read passage independently Students answer questions

Teaching Sequence:	Extension	
words taught. Model reading Ask questions about passage using various strategies and model responses	help each other to answer questions.	independently

Reading Component: Phonemic Awareness, Phonics, Vocabulary, Fluency Comprehension

Teaching Sequence:	Evaluation	
Aim:	*To allow students to practice independent reading	
I Do Teacher shows how it's done	**We Do** Teacher and students do it together	**You Do** Students show the teacher how it's done
Corrective should be minor and one-on-one Delay feedback – Let them self-correct Circulate during seatwork, monitoring students with short contacts **Do Not Go Over Work And Give Answers.** **Collect** work to see students who have mastered and those who still need further help.	Collaboration does not happen at this teaching sequence	Students are completing task independently.

Easy Reader Level B

Pre Assessment Scoring Sheet

Name: _________________   Date: _________________

Instruction: Tick each correct response. Record the errors made on the line to correct errors during instruction.

1. fat _______________   11. nap _______________

2. Tim_______________   12. doll _______________

3. pen _______________   13. mix_______________

4. jet _______________   14. yell_______________

5. Zac_______________   15. wig_______________

6. quit_______________   16. lid _______________

7. vet _______________   17. gun _______________

8. rip _______________   18. box_______________

9. cut _______________   19. sat _______________

10. kit_______________   20. hen_______________

Number correct: _____ Speed: Slow☐ Moderate☐ Fast☐

Areas of Strength:

____

____

Areas of Need & Plan for Intervention:

____

____

Pre Assessment Record Sheet

Grade/Class: _____________________ Teacher: _____________________

Name of Child	Total Score	Speed S, M, F

Easy Reader Level B

Phonetic Words Assessment Progress Sheet

Grade/Class: _______   Teacher: _______________   Date: _______________

Name of Child	Assessment 1		Assessment 2		Assessment 3		Assessment 4		Assessment 5	
	Total Score	Speed S, M, F	Total Score	Speed S, M, F	Total Score	Speed S, M, F	Total Score	Speed S, M, F	Total Score	Speed S, M, F

High-Frequency Words Assessment Progress Sheet

Grade/Class: _______   Teacher: _________________   Date: _________________

Name of Child	Assessment 1		Assessment 2		Assessment 3		Assessment 4		Assessment 5	
	Total Score	Speed S, M, F	Total Score	Speed S, M, F	Total Score	Speed S, M, F	Total Score	Speed S, M, F	Total Score	Speed S, M, F